EXODUS

The Second Book of Mose

This WORKBOOK is designed to help assist the diligent study of those who would know the Word of God. It is written in a format that REQUIRES reading of the text from the Authorized King James Version of the Holy Scriptures.

The King James Bible correctly fills all of the available "blanks" in this workbook.

Other workbooks are available by contacting us:

By FAITH Publications
85 Hendersonville Hwy.
Walterboro, SC 29488

(843) 538-2269

www.faithbaptistchurch.us

publications@faithbaptistchurch.us

EXODUS

Exodus 1:1-40:38 (KJV)

Now these *are* the names of the children of Israel, which came into Egypt; every man and his household came with _____. ² _____, _____, _____, and _____, ³ _____, _____, and _____, ⁴ _____, and _____, _____, and _____. ⁵And all the souls that came out of the loins of Jacob were seventy souls: for _____ was in Egypt *already*. ⁶And Joseph died, and all his brethren, and all that generation.

⁷And the children of Israel were fruitful, and increased abundantly, and multiplied, and waxed exceeding mighty; and the land was filled with them. ⁸Now there arose up a new king over _____, which knew not _____. ⁹And he said unto his people, Behold, the people of the children of Israel *are* more and mightier than we: ¹⁰Come on, let us deal wisely with them; lest they _____, and it come to pass, that, when there falleth out any war, they join also unto our enemies, and fight against us, and *so* get them up out of the land. ¹¹Therefore they did set over them _____ to afflict them with their burdens. And they built for Pharaoh _____ _____, Pithom and Raamses. ¹²But the more they afflicted them, the more they multiplied and grew. And they were grieved because of the children of Israel. ¹³And the Egyptians made the children of Israel to serve with rigour: ¹⁴And they made their lives bitter with hard _____, in morter, and in brick, and in all manner of service in the field: all their service, wherein they made them serve, *was* with rigour.

¹⁵And the king of Egypt spake to the Hebrew _____, of which the name of the one *was* Shiphrah, and the name of the other Puah: ¹⁶And he said, When ye do the office of a midwife to the Hebrew women, and see *them* upon the stools; if it *be* a _____, then ye shall _____ him: but if it *be* a _____, then she shall _____. ¹⁷But the midwives _____ God, and did _____ as the king of Egypt commanded them, but saved the men children alive. ¹⁸And the king of Egypt called for the midwives, and said unto them, Why have ye done this thing, and have saved the men children alive? ¹⁹And the midwives said unto Pharaoh, Because the Hebrew women *are* not as the Egyptian women; for they *are* lively, and are delivered ere the midwives come in unto them. ²⁰Therefore God dealt well with the midwives: and the people multiplied, and waxed very mighty. ²¹And it came to pass, because the midwives feared God, that he made them houses. ²²And Pharaoh charged all his people, saying, Every _____ that is born ye shall cast into the river, and every _____ ye shall save alive.

²:¹And there went a man of the house of _____, and took *to wife* a daughter of _____. ²And the woman conceived, and bare a son: and when she saw him that he *was a* _____ *child,* she hid him _____ months. ³And when she could not longer hide him, she took for him an _____ of _____, and daubed it with slime and with pitch, and put the child therein; and she laid *it* in the flags by the river's brink. ⁴And his _____ stood afar off, to wit what would be done to him.

⁵And the _____ of _____ came down to wash *herself* at the river; and her maidens walked along by the river's side; and when she saw the ark among the flags, she sent her maid to fetch it. ⁶And when she had opened *it,* she saw the child: and, behold, the babe wept. And she had compassion on him, and said, This *is one* of the _____ children. ⁷Then said his sister to Pharaoh's daughter, Shall I go and call to thee a _____ of the Hebrew women, that she may nurse the child for thee? ⁸And Pharaoh's daughter said to her, Go. And the maid went and called the child's _____.

                    By Faith Publications

⁹And Pharaoh's daughter said unto her, Take this child away, and _____ it for me, and I will give *thee* thy _____. And the woman took the child, and nursed it. ¹⁰And the child grew, and she brought him unto Pharaoh's daughter, and he became her son. And she called his name _____: and she said, Because I _____ him out of the water.

¹¹And it came to pass in those days, when Moses was _____, that he went out unto his brethren, and looked on their burdens: and he spied an _____ smiting an _____, one of his _____. ¹²And he looked this way and that way, and when he saw that *there was* no man, he _____ the Egyptian, and _____ him in the _____. ¹³And when he went out the second day, behold, two men of the Hebrews strove together: and he said to him that did the wrong, Wherefore smitest thou thy fellow? ¹⁴And he said, Who made thee a prince and a judge over us? intendest thou to kill me, as thou killedst the Egyptian? And Moses feared, and said, Surely this thing is known. ¹⁵Now when Pharaoh heard this thing, he sought to _____ Moses. But Moses fled from the face of Pharaoh, and dwelt in the land of _____: and he sat down by a _____. ¹⁶Now the priest of Midian had _____ daughters: and they came and drew *water,* and filled the troughs to water their father's flock. ¹⁷And the shepherds came and drove them away: but Moses stood up and helped them, and watered their flock. ¹⁸And when they came to _____ their father, he said, How *is it that* ye are come so soon to day? ¹⁹And they said, An Egyptian delivered us out of the hand of the shepherds, and also drew *water* enough for us, and watered the flock. ²⁰And he said unto his daughters, And where *is* he? why *is it that* ye have left the man? call him, that he may eat bread. ²¹And Moses was content to dwell with the man: and he gave Moses _____ his daughter. ²²And she bare *him* a son, and he called his name _____: for he said, I have been a stranger in a strange land.

²³And it came to pass in process of time, that the king of Egypt died: and the children of Israel sighed by reason of the bondage, and they _____, and their cry came up unto God by reason of the bondage. ²⁴And God _____ their groaning, and God _____ his covenant with Abraham, with Isaac, and with Jacob. ²⁵And God _____ upon the children of Israel, and God had _____ unto *them.*

³:¹Now Moses kept the flock of _____ his father in law, the priest of Midian: and he led the flock to the backside of the _____, and came to the _____ of God, *even* to _____. ²And the angel of the LORD appeared unto him in a flame of _____ out of the midst of a _____: and he looked, and, behold, the bush _____ with fire, and the bush *was* not _____. ³And Moses said, I will now turn aside, and see this great sight, why the bush is not burnt. ⁴And when the LORD saw that he turned aside to see, God called unto him out of the midst of the bush, and said, Moses, Moses. And he said, Here *am* I. ⁵And he said, Draw not nigh hither: put off thy _____ from _____ thy _____, for the _____ whereon thou _____ is _____ ground. ⁶Moreover he said, I *am* the God of thy _____, the God of Abraham, the God of Isaac, and the God of Jacob. And Moses hid his face; for he was _____ to look upon God.

⁷And the LORD said, I have surely seen the affliction of my people which *are* in Egypt, and have heard their cry by reason of their taskmasters; for I know their _____; ⁸And I am come down to _____ them out of the hand of the Egyptians, and to bring them up out of that land unto a good land and a large, unto a land flowing with

_____ and _____; unto the place of the Canaanites, and the Hittites, and the Amorites, and the Perizzites, and the Hivites, and the Jebusites. ⁹Now therefore, behold, the cry of the children of Israel is come unto me: and I have also seen the oppression wherewith the Egyptians oppress them. ¹⁰Come now therefore, and I will send thee unto Pharaoh, that thou mayest bring forth my people the children of Israel out of Egypt.

¹¹And Moses said unto God, Who *am* I, that I should go unto Pharaoh, and that I should bring forth the children of Israel out of Egypt? ¹²And he said, Certainly I will be with thee; and this *shall be* a token unto thee, that I have sent thee: When thou hast brought forth the people out of Egypt, ye shall _____ God upon this _____. ¹³And Moses said unto God, Behold, *when* I come unto the children of Israel, and shall say unto them, The God of your fathers hath sent me unto you; and they shall say to me, What is his name? what shall I say unto them? ¹⁴And God said unto Moses, _____: and he said, Thus shalt thou say unto the children of Israel, I AM hath sent me unto you. ¹⁵And God said moreover unto Moses, Thus shalt thou say unto the children of Israel, The LORD God of your fathers, the God of Abraham, the God of Isaac, and the God of Jacob, hath sent me unto you: this *is* my name for ever, and this *is* my memorial unto all generations. ¹⁶Go, and gather the elders of Israel together, and say unto them, The LORD God of your fathers, the God of Abraham, of Isaac, and of Jacob, appeared unto me, saying, I have surely visited you, and *seen* that which is done to you in Egypt: ¹⁷And I have said, I will bring you up out of the affliction of Egypt unto the land of the Canaanites, and the Hittites, and the Amorites, and the Perizzites, and the Hivites, and the Jebusites, unto a land flowing with milk and honey. ¹⁸And they shall hearken to thy voice: and thou shalt come, thou and the elders of Israel, unto the king of Egypt, and ye shall say unto him, The LORD God of the Hebrews hath met with us: and now let us go, we beseech thee, three days' journey into the wilderness, that we may sacrifice to the LORD our God.

¹⁹And I am sure that the king of Egypt will _____ let you go, no, not by a mighty hand. ²⁰And I will stretch out my hand, and _____ Egypt with all my _____ which I will do in the midst thereof: and _____ that he will let you go. ²¹And I will give this people _____ in the sight of the Egyptians: and it shall come to pass, that, when ye go, ye shall not go empty: ²²But every woman shall borrow of her neighbour, and of her that sojourneth in her house, jewels of silver, and jewels of gold, and raiment: and ye shall put *them* upon your sons, and upon your daughters; and ye shall spoil the Egyptians.

⁴:¹And Moses answered and said, But, behold, they will not believe me, nor hearken unto my voice: for they will say, The LORD hath not appeared unto thee. ²And the LORD said unto him, What *is* that in thine hand? And he said, A _____. ³And he said, Cast it on the ground. And he cast it on the ground, and it became a _____; and Moses fled from before it. ⁴And the LORD said unto Moses, Put forth thine hand, and take it by the _____. And he put forth his hand, and caught it, and it became a rod in his hand: ⁵That they may believe that the LORD God of their fathers, the God of Abraham, the God of Isaac, and the God of Jacob, hath appeared unto thee.

⁶And the LORD said furthermore unto him, Put now thine _____ into thy _____. And he put his hand into his bosom: and when he took it out, behold, his hand *was* _____ as _____. ⁷And he said, Put thine hand into thy bosom again. And he put his hand into his bosom again; and plucked it out of his bosom, and, behold, it

was turned again as his *other* flesh. ⁸And it shall come to pass, if they will not believe thee, neither hearken to the voice of the first sign, that they will believe the voice of the latter sign. ⁹And it shall come to pass, if they will not believe also these two signs, neither hearken unto thy voice, that thou shalt take of the _____ of the _____, and pour *it* upon the dry *land:* and the water which thou takest out of the river shall become _____ upon the dry *land.*

¹⁰And Moses said unto the LORD, O my Lord, I *am* not _____, neither heretofore, nor since thou hast spoken unto thy servant: but I *am* _____ of _____, and of a slow tongue. ¹¹And the LORD said unto him, Who hath made man's _____? or who maketh the _____, or _____, or the _____, or the _____? have not _____ the LORD? ¹²Now therefore go, and I will be with thy mouth, and _____ thee what thou shalt _____. ¹³And he said, O my Lord, send, I pray thee, by the hand *of him whom* thou wilt send. ¹⁴And the _____ of the LORD was kindled against Moses, and he said, *Is* not _____ the Levite thy _____? I know that he can speak well. And also, behold, he cometh forth to meet thee: and when he seeth thee, he will be _____ in his heart. ¹⁵And thou shalt speak unto him, and put words in his mouth: and I will _____ with thy mouth, and with his mouth, and will _____ you what ye shall do. ¹⁶And he shall be thy _____ unto the people: and he shall be, *even* he shall be to thee instead of a _____, and thou shalt be to him instead of _____. ¹⁷And thou shalt take this _____ in thine hand, wherewith thou shalt do _____.

¹⁸And Moses went and returned to _____ his father in law, and said unto him, Let me go, I pray thee, and return unto my brethren which *are* in _____, and see whether they be yet _____. And Jethro said to Moses, Go in peace. ¹⁹And the LORD said unto Moses in Midian, Go, return into Egypt: for all the men are _____ which sought thy life. ²⁰And Moses took his _____ and his _____, and set them upon an ass, and he returned to the land of Egypt: and Moses took the rod of God in his hand. ²¹And the LORD said unto Moses, When thou goest to return into Egypt, see that thou do all those wonders before Pharaoh, which I have put in thine hand: but I will _____ his heart, that he shall _____ let the people go. ²²And thou shalt say unto Pharaoh, Thus saith the _____, Israel *is* my _____, *even* my firstborn: ²³And I say unto thee, Let my son go, that he may serve me: and if thou refuse to let him go, behold, I will _____ thy _____, *even* thy firstborn.

²⁴And it came to pass by the way in the inn, that the LORD met him, and sought to kill him. ²⁵Then _____ took a sharp _____, and cut off the foreskin of her son, and cast *it* at his feet, and said, Surely a _____ husband *art* thou to me. ²⁶So he let him go: then she said, A bloody husband *thou art,* because of the _____.

²⁷And the LORD said to _____, Go into the wilderness to meet Moses. And he went, and met him in the _____ of God, and kissed him. ²⁸And Moses told Aaron all the words of the LORD who had sent him, and all the _____ which he had commanded him.

²⁹And Moses and Aaron went and gathered together all the _____ of the children of Israel: ³⁰And Aaron spake all the words which the LORD had spoken unto Moses, and did the signs in the sight of the people. ³¹And the people _____: and when they heard that the LORD had visited the children of Israel, and that he had looked upon their affliction, then they bowed their heads and _____.

5:1And afterward Moses and Aaron went in, and told Pharaoh, Thus saith the LORD God of Israel, Let my people go, that they may hold a feast unto me in the wilderness. 2And Pharaoh said, _____ *is* the _____, that I should _____ his voice to let Israel go? I know _____ the LORD, neither will I let Israel _____. 3And they said, The God of the _____ hath met with us: let us go, we pray thee, three days' journey into the desert, and sacrifice unto the LORD our God; lest he fall upon us with _____, or with the sword. 4And the king of Egypt said unto them, Wherefore do ye, Moses and Aaron, let the people from their _____? get you unto your _____. 5And Pharaoh said, Behold, the people of the land now *are* many, and ye make them rest from their burdens. 6And Pharaoh commanded the same day the _____ of the people, and their officers, saying, 7Ye shall no more give the people _____ to make brick, as heretofore: let them go and _____ straw for themselves. 8And the _____ of the bricks, which they did make heretofore, ye shall lay upon them; ye shall not _____ *ought* thereof: for they *be* _____; therefore they cry, saying, Let us go *and* sacrifice to our God. 9Let there more work be laid upon the men, that they may labour therein; and let them not regard vain words.

10And the taskmasters of the people went out, and their officers, and they spake to the people, saying, Thus saith Pharaoh, I will not give you straw. 11Go ye, get you straw where ye can find it: yet not ought of your work shall be diminished. 12So the people were scattered abroad throughout all the land of Egypt to gather _____ instead of straw. 13And the taskmasters hasted *them,* saying, Fulfil your works, *your* daily tasks, as when there was straw. 14And the officers of the children of Israel, which Pharaoh's taskmasters had set over them, were _____, *and* demanded, Wherefore have ye not fulfilled your task in making brick both yesterday and to day, as heretofore?

15Then the officers of the children of Israel came and cried unto Pharaoh, saying, Wherefore dealest thou thus with thy servants? 16There is no straw given unto thy servants, and they say to us, Make _____: and, behold, thy servants *are* _____; but the fault *is* in thine own people. 17But he said, Ye *are* _____, *ye are* idle: therefore ye say, Let us go *and* do sacrifice to the LORD. 18Go therefore now, *and* work; for there shall no straw be given you, yet shall ye deliver the tale of bricks. 19And the officers of the children of Israel did see *that* they *were* in evil *case,* after it was said, Ye shall not minish *ought* from your bricks of your daily task.

20And they met Moses and Aaron, who stood in the way, as they came forth from Pharaoh: 21And they said unto them, The LORD look upon you, and judge; because ye have made our savour to be abhorred in the eyes of Pharaoh, and in the eyes of his servants, to put a sword in their hand to _____ us. 22And Moses returned unto the LORD, and said, Lord, wherefore hast thou *so* evil entreated this people? why *is* it *that* thou hast sent me? 23For since I came to Pharaoh to speak in thy name, he hath done evil to this people; neither hast thou delivered thy people at all.

6:1Then the LORD said unto Moses, Now shalt thou see what I will _____ to Pharaoh: for with a strong _____ shall he let them go, and with a strong hand shall he _____ them out of his land. 2And God spake unto Moses, and said unto him, I *am* the LORD: 3And I appeared unto _____, unto _____, and unto _____, by *the name of* _____, but by my name _____ was I not known to them. 4And I have also established my _____ with them, to give them the land of _____, the land of their pilgrimage, wherein they were strangers.

⁵And I have also heard the _____ of the children of Israel, whom the Egyptians keep in bondage; and I have _____ my covenant. ⁶Wherefore say unto the children of Israel, I *am* the L ORD, and I will bring you _____ from under the burdens of the Egyptians, and I will rid you out of their _____, and I will _____ you with a _____ out arm, and with great _____: ⁷And I will _____ you to me for a people, and I will be to you a _____: and ye shall know that I *am* the _____ your God, which _____ you _____ from _____ the _____ of the Egyptians. ⁸And I will bring you in unto the land, concerning the which I did swear to give it to Abraham, to Isaac, and to Jacob; and I will give it you for an _____ : _____ _____ the L ORD.

⁹And Moses spake so unto the children of Israel: but they hearkened _____ unto Moses for _____ of spirit, and for cruel _____. ¹⁰And the L ORD spake unto Moses, saying, ¹¹Go in, speak unto Pharaoh king of Egypt, that he let the children of Israel go out of his land. ¹²And Moses spake before the L ORD, saying, Behold, the children of Israel have not hearkened unto me; how then shall Pharaoh hear me, who *am* of uncircumcised lips? ¹³And the L ORD spake unto Moses and unto Aaron, and gave them a charge unto the children of Israel, and unto Pharaoh king of Egypt, to bring the children of Israel out of the land of Egypt.

¹⁴These *be* the heads of their fathers' houses: The sons of _____ the firstborn of Israel; Hanoch, and Pallu, Hezron, and Carmi: these *be* the families of Reuben. ¹⁵And the sons of _____; Jemuel, and Jamin, and Ohad, and Jachin, and Zohar, and Shaul the son of a Canaanitish woman: these *are* the families of Simeon.

¹⁶And these *are* the names of the sons of _____ according to their generations; Gershon, and Kohath, and Merari: and the years of the life of Levi *were* an hundred thirty and seven years. ¹⁷The sons of Gershon; Libni, and Shimi, according to their families. ¹⁸And the sons of Kohath; Amram, and Izhar, and Hebron, and Uzziel: and the years of the life of Kohath *were* an hundred thirty and three years. ¹⁹And the sons of Merari; Mahali and Mushi: these *are* the families of Levi according to their generations. ²⁰And _____ took him _____ his father's sister to wife; and she bare him _____ and _____ : and the years of the life of Amram *were* an hundred and thirty and seven years.

²¹And the sons of Izhar; Korah, and Nepheg, and Zichri. ²²And the sons of Uzziel; Mishael, and Elzaphan, and Zithri. ²³And _____ took him _____, daughter of Amminadab, sister of Naashon, to wife; and she bare him _____, and _____, _____, and _____. ²⁴And the sons of Korah; Assir, and Elkanah, and Abiasaph: these *are* the families of the Korhites. ²⁵And _____ Aaron's son took him *one* of the daughters of _____ to wife; and she bare him _____: these *are* the heads of the fathers of the Levites according to their families. ²⁶These *are* that Aaron and Moses, to whom the L ORD said, Bring out the _____ of Israel from the land of Egypt according to their armies. ²⁷These *are* they which spake to Pharaoh king of Egypt, to bring out the children of Israel from Egypt: these *are* that Moses and Aaron.

²⁸And it came to pass on the day *when* the L ORD spake unto Moses in the land of Egypt, ²⁹That the L ORD spake unto Moses, saying, I *am* the L ORD: speak thou unto Pharaoh king of Egypt all that I say unto thee. ³⁰And Moses said before the L ORD, Behold, I *am* of uncircumcised lips, and how shall Pharaoh hearken unto me?

7:1And the LORD said unto Moses, See, I have made thee a _____ to Pharaoh: and Aaron thy brother shall be thy _____. 2Thou shalt speak all that I _____ thee: and Aaron thy brother shall speak unto Pharaoh, that he _____ the children of Israel out of his land. 3And I will _____ Pharaoh's _____, and multiply my signs and my wonders in the land of Egypt. 4But Pharaoh shall _____ hearken unto you, that I may _____ my _____ upon Egypt, and bring forth mine _____, *and* my people the children of Israel, out of the land of Egypt by great judgments. 5And the Egyptians shall _____ that I *am* the LORD, when I stretch forth mine hand upon Egypt, and bring out the children of Israel from among them. 6And Moses and Aaron _____ as the LORD _____ them, so _____ they. 7And Moses *was* _____ years old, and Aaron fourscore and _____ years old, when they spake unto Pharaoh.

8And the LORD spake unto Moses and unto Aaron, saying, 9When Pharaoh shall speak unto you, saying, Shew a miracle for you: then thou shalt say unto Aaron, Take thy rod, and cast *it* before Pharaoh, *and* it shall become a _____.

10And Moses and Aaron went in unto Pharaoh, and they did so as the LORD had commanded: and Aaron cast down his rod before Pharaoh, and before his servants, and it became a serpent. 11Then Pharaoh also called the wise men and the _____: now the _____ of Egypt, they also did in like manner with their _____. 12For they cast down every man his rod, and they became serpents: but Aaron's rod _____ up their rods. 13And he _____ Pharaoh's heart, that he hearkened not unto them; as the LORD had said.

14And the LORD said unto Moses, Pharaoh's heart *is* hardened, he _____ to let the people go. 15Get thee unto Pharaoh in the _____; lo, he goeth out unto the water; and thou shalt stand by the river's brink against he come; and the rod which was turned to a serpent shalt thou take in thine hand. 16And thou shalt say unto him, The LORD God of the Hebrews hath sent me unto thee, saying, Let my people go, that they may serve me in the wilderness: and, behold, hitherto thou wouldest not hear. 17Thus saith the LORD, In this thou shalt know that I *am* the LORD: behold, I will _____ with the _____ that *is* in mine hand upon the _____ which *are* in the river, and they shall be turned to _____. 18And the fish that *is* in the river shall _____, and the river shall _____; and the Egyptians shall lothe to drink of the water of the river.

19And the LORD spake unto Moses, Say unto Aaron, Take thy rod, and stretch out thine hand upon the waters of Egypt, upon their streams, upon their rivers, and upon their ponds, and upon all their pools of water, that they may become _____; and *that* there may be blood throughout all the land of Egypt, both in *vessels of* wood, and in *vessels of* stone. 20And Moses and Aaron did so, as the LORD commanded; and he lifted up the rod, and smote the waters that *were* in the river, in the sight of Pharaoh, and in the sight of his servants; and all the waters that *were* in the river were turned to blood. 21And the fish that *was* in the river died; and the river stank, and the Egyptians could not drink of the water of the river; and there was blood throughout all the land of Egypt. 22And the magicians of Egypt did so with their enchantments: and Pharaoh's heart was _____, _____ did he _____ unto them; as the LORD had said. 23And Pharaoh turned and went into his house, neither did he set his heart to this also. 24And all the Egyptians digged round about the river for water to drink; for they could not drink of the water of the river. ²⁵And _____ days were fulfilled, after that the LORD had smitten the river.

⁸:¹And the LORD spake unto Moses, Go unto Pharaoh, and say unto him, Thus saith the LORD, Let my people go, that they may serve me. ²And if thou refuse to let *them* go, behold, I will _____ all thy borders with _____ : ³And the river shall bring forth frogs abundantly, which shall go up and come into thine house, and into thy bedchamber, and upon thy bed, and into the house of thy servants, and upon thy people, and into thine ovens, and into thy kneadingtroughs: ⁴And the frogs shall come up both on thee, and upon thy people, and upon all thy servants.

⁵And the LORD spake unto Moses, Say unto Aaron, Stretch forth thine hand with thy rod over the streams, over the rivers, and over the ponds, and cause frogs to come up upon the land of Egypt. ⁶And Aaron stretched out his hand over the waters of Egypt; and the frogs came up, and covered the land of Egypt. ⁷And the _____ did so with their enchantments, and brought up frogs upon the land of Egypt.

⁸Then Pharaoh _____ for Moses and Aaron, and said, Intreat the _____ , that he may take _____ the frogs from me, and from my people; and I will let the people go, that they may do sacrifice unto the LORD. ⁹And Moses said unto Pharaoh, _____ over me: _____ shall I intreat for thee, and for thy servants, and for thy people, to destroy the frogs from thee and thy houses, *that* they may remain in the river only? ¹⁰And he said, _____ . And he said, *Be it* according to thy word: that thou mayest know that *there is* _____ like unto the LORD our God. ¹¹And the frogs shall depart from thee, and from thy houses, and from thy servants, and from thy people; they shall remain in the river only. ¹²And Moses and Aaron went out from Pharaoh: and Moses cried unto the LORD because of the frogs which he had brought against Pharaoh. ¹³And the LORD did according to the word of Moses; and the frogs _____ out of the houses, out of the villages, and out of the fields. ¹⁴And they gathered them together upon heaps: and the land _____ . ¹⁵But when Pharaoh saw that there was _____ , he _____ his heart, and hearkened _____ unto them; as the LORD had said.

¹⁶And the LORD said unto Moses, Say unto Aaron, Stretch out thy _____ , and smite the dust of the land, that it may become _____ throughout all the land of Egypt. ¹⁷And they did so; for Aaron stretched out his hand with his rod, and smote the _____ of the earth, and it became lice in man, and in beast; all the dust of the land became lice throughout all the land of Egypt. ¹⁸And the _____ did so with their _____ to bring forth lice, but they could _____ : so there were lice upon man, and upon beast. ¹⁹Then the magicians said unto Pharaoh, This *is* the _____ of God: and Pharaoh's heart was _____ , and he hearkened _____ unto them; as the LORD had said.

²⁰And the LORD said unto Moses, Rise up early in the morning, and stand before Pharaoh; lo, he cometh forth to the water; and say unto him, Thus saith the LORD, Let my people go, that they may serve me. ²¹Else, if thou wilt not let my people go, behold, I will send _____ *of* _____ upon thee, and upon thy servants, and upon thy people, and into thy houses: and the houses of the Egyptians shall be full of _____ *of* _____ , and also the ground whereon they *are.* ²²And I will sever in that day the land of Goshen, in which my people dwell, that no swarms *of flies* shall be there; to the end thou mayest know that I *am* the LORD in the midst of the earth. ²³And I will put a

_____ between my people and thy people: to morrow shall this sign be. ²⁴And the LORD did so; and there came a grievous swarm *of flies* into the house of Pharaoh, and *into* his servants' houses, and into all the land of Egypt: the land was _____ by reason of the swarm *of flies*.

²⁵And Pharaoh called for Moses and for Aaron, and said, Go ye, sacrifice to your God _____ the land. ²⁶And Moses said, It is not meet so to do; for we shall sacrifice the abomination of the Egyptians to the LORD our God: lo, shall we sacrifice the abomination of the Egyptians before their eyes, and will they not stone us? ²⁷We will go three days' journey into the wilderness, and sacrifice to the LORD our God, _____ he shall _____ us. ²⁸And Pharaoh said, I will let you go, that ye may sacrifice to the LORD your God in the wilderness; only ye shall not go very far away: intreat for me. ²⁹And Moses said, Behold, I go out from thee, and I will intreat the LORD that the swarms *of flies* may depart from Pharaoh, from his servants, and from his people, to morrow: but let not Pharaoh deal _____ any more in not letting the people go to sacrifice to the LORD. ³⁰And Moses went out from Pharaoh, and intreated the LORD. ³¹And the LORD did according to the word of Moses; and he removed the swarms *of flies* from Pharaoh, from his servants, and from his people; there remained not one. ³²And Pharaoh _____ his _____ at this time also, _____ would he let the people go.

^{9:1}Then the LORD said unto Moses, Go in unto Pharaoh, and tell him, Thus saith the LORD God of the Hebrews, Let my people go, that they may serve me. ²For if thou refuse to let *them* go, and wilt hold them still, ³Behold, the hand of the LORD is upon thy _____ which *is* in the field, upon the horses, upon the asses, upon the camels, upon the oxen, and upon the sheep: *there shall be* a very grievous _____. ⁴And the LORD shall sever between the cattle of _____ and the cattle of _____: and there shall _____ die of all *that is* the children's of Israel. ⁵And the LORD appointed a set time, saying, To morrow the LORD shall do this thing in the land. ⁶And the LORD did that thing on the morrow, and _____ the cattle of Egypt died: but of the cattle of the children of Israel died not _____. ⁷And Pharaoh sent, and, behold, there was not one of the cattle of the Israelites dead. And the heart of Pharaoh was _____, and he did not let the people go.

⁸And the LORD said unto Moses and unto Aaron, Take to you handfuls of _____ of the furnace, and let Moses sprinkle it toward the heaven in the sight of Pharaoh. ⁹And it shall become small dust in all the land of Egypt, and shall be a _____ breaking forth *with* blains upon man, and upon beast, throughout all the land of Egypt. ¹⁰And they took ashes of the furnace, and stood before Pharaoh; and Moses sprinkled it up toward heaven; and it became a boil breaking forth *with* blains upon man, and upon beast. ¹¹And the _____ could _____ _____ before Moses because of the boils; for the boil was upon the magicians, and upon all the Egyptians. ¹²And the LORD hardened the heart of Pharaoh, and he hearkened not unto them; as the LORD had spoken unto Moses.

¹³And the LORD said unto Moses, Rise up early in the morning, and stand before Pharaoh, and say unto him, Thus saith the LORD God of the Hebrews, Let my people go, that they may serve me. ¹⁴For I will at this time send _____ my _____ upon thine _____, and upon thy _____, and upon thy _____; that thou mayest _____ that *there is* _____ like me in all the _____. ¹⁵For now I will stretch out my hand, that I may smite thee and thy people with pestilence; and thou

shalt be cut off from the earth. [16]And in very deed for this *cause* have I raised thee up, for to shew *in* thee my power; and that my name may be declared throughout all the earth. [17]As yet exaltest thou thyself against my people, that thou wilt not let them go? [18]Behold, to morrow about this time I will cause it to rain a very grievous _____, such as hath not been in Egypt since the foundation thereof even until now. [19]Send therefore now, *and* gather thy cattle, and all that thou hast in the field; *for upon* every man and beast which shall be found in the field, and shall not be brought home, the hail shall come down upon them, and they shall die. [20]He that _____ the _____ of the LORD among the servants of Pharaoh made his servants and his cattle flee into the houses: [21]And he that regarded _____ the word of the LORD _____ his servants and his cattle in the field.

[22]And the LORD said unto Moses, Stretch forth thine hand toward heaven, that there may be _____ in all the land of Egypt, upon man, and upon beast, and upon every herb of the field, throughout the land of Egypt. [23]And Moses stretched forth his rod toward heaven: and the LORD sent thunder and hail, and the _____ ran along upon the ground; and the LORD rained hail upon the land of Egypt. [24]So there was hail, and fire mingled with the hail, very grievous, such as there was none like it in all the land of Egypt since it became a nation. [25]And the hail smote throughout all the land of Egypt all that *was* in the field, both man and beast; and the hail smote every herb of the field, and brake every tree of the field. [26]Only in the land of _____, where the children of Israel *were,* was there _____ hail.

[27]And Pharaoh sent, and called for Moses and Aaron, and said unto them, I have _____ _____ _____: the LORD *is* _____, and I and my people *are* _____. [28]Intreat the LORD (for *it is* _____) that there be no *more* mighty thunderings and hail; and I will let you go, and ye shall stay no longer. [29]And Moses said unto him, As soon as I am gone out of the city, I will spread abroad my hands unto the LORD; *and* the thunder shall cease, neither shall there be any more hail; that thou mayest know how that the earth *is* the LORD'S. [30]But as for thee and thy servants, I know that ye will _____ yet fear the LORD God. [31]And the flax and the barley was smitten: for the barley was in the ear, and the flax *was* bolled. [32]But the wheat and the rie were not smitten: for they *were* not grown up. [33]And Moses went out of the city from Pharaoh, and spread abroad his hands unto the LORD: and the thunders and hail ceased, and the rain was not poured upon the earth. [34]And when Pharaoh saw that the rain and the hail and the thunders were ceased, he _____ yet _____, and hardened his heart, he and his servants. [35]And the heart of Pharaoh was hardened, neither would he let the children of Israel go; as the LORD had spoken by Moses.

[10:1]And the LORD said unto Moses, Go in unto Pharaoh: for I have hardened his heart, and the heart of his servants, that I might shew these my signs before him: [2]And that thou mayest _____ in the ears of thy son, and of thy son's son, what things I have wrought in Egypt, and my signs which I have done among them; that ye may _____ how that I *am* the LORD. [3]And Moses and Aaron came in unto Pharaoh, and said unto him, Thus saith the LORD God of the Hebrews, How long wilt thou refuse to humble thyself before me? let my people go, that they may serve me. [4]Else, if thou refuse to let my people go, behold, to morrow will I bring the _____ into thy coast: [5]And they shall cover the face of the earth, that one cannot be able to see the earth: and they shall eat the residue of that which is escaped, which remaineth unto you from the hail, and shall eat every tree which groweth for you out of the field: ⁶And they shall fill thy houses, and the houses of all thy servants, and the houses of all the Egyptians; which neither thy fathers, nor thy fathers' fathers have seen, since the day that they were upon the earth unto this day. And he turned himself, and went out from Pharaoh. ⁷And Pharaoh's _____ said unto him, How long shall this man be a snare unto us? let the men go, that they may serve the LORD their God: knowest thou not yet that Egypt is _____? ⁸And Moses and Aaron were brought again unto Pharaoh: and he said unto them, Go, serve the LORD your God: *but* who *are* they that shall go? ⁹And Moses said, We will go with our young and with our old, with our sons and with our daughters, with our flocks and with our herds will we go; for we *must hold* a feast unto the LORD. ¹⁰And he said unto them, Let the LORD be so with you, as I will let you go, and your little ones: look *to it;* for evil *is* before you. ¹¹Not so: go now ye *that are* _____, and serve the LORD; for that ye did desire. And they were _____ out from Pharaoh's presence.

¹²And the LORD said unto Moses, Stretch out thine hand over the land of Egypt for the locusts, that they may come up upon the land of Egypt, and eat every herb of the land, *even* all that the hail hath left. ¹³And Moses stretched forth his rod over the land of Egypt, and the LORD brought an east wind upon the land all that day, and all *that* night; *and* when it was morning, the east wind brought the locusts. ¹⁴And the locusts went up over all the land of Egypt, and rested in all the coasts of Egypt: very grievous *were they;* before them there were no such locusts as they, neither after them shall be such. ¹⁵For they covered the face of the whole earth, so that the land was darkened; and they did eat every herb of the land, and all the fruit of the trees which the hail had left: and there remained not any green thing in the trees, or in the herbs of the field, through all the land of Egypt.

¹⁶Then Pharaoh called for Moses and Aaron in haste; and he said, I have sinned against the _____ your God, and against _____. ¹⁷Now therefore _____, I pray thee, my sin only this _____, and intreat the LORD your God, that he may take away from me this death only. ¹⁸And he went out from Pharaoh, and intreated the LORD. ¹⁹And the LORD turned a mighty strong west wind, which took away the locusts, and cast them into the Red sea; there remained not one locust in all the coasts of Egypt. ²⁰But the LORD hardened Pharaoh's heart, so that he would not let the children of Israel go.

²¹And the LORD said unto Moses, Stretch out thine hand toward heaven, that there may be _____ over the land of Egypt, even darkness *which* may be _____. ²²And Moses stretched forth his hand toward heaven; and there was a _____ darkness in all the land of Egypt _____ days: ²³They saw not one another, neither rose any from his place for three days: but all the children of Israel had _____ in their dwellings.

²⁴And Pharaoh called unto Moses, and said, Go ye, serve the LORD; only let your flocks and your herds be stayed: let your little ones also go with you. ²⁵And Moses said, Thou must give us also sacrifices and burnt offerings, that we may sacrifice unto the LORD our God. ²⁶Our cattle also shall go with us; there shall not an _____ be left behind; for thereof must we take to serve the LORD our God; and we know not with what we must serve the LORD, until we come thither.

²⁷But the LORD hardened Pharaoh's heart, and he would not let them go. ²⁸And Pharaoh said unto him, Get thee from me, take heed to thyself, see my face no more; for in *that* day thou seest my face thou shalt _____. ²⁹And Moses said, Thou hast spoken well, I will see thy _____ again no more.

11:1And the LORD said unto Moses, Yet will I bring _____ plague *more* upon Pharaoh, and upon Egypt; afterwards he _____ let you go hence: when he shall let *you* go, he shall surely _____ you out hence altogether. 2Speak now in the ears of the people, and let every man _____ of his neighbour, and every woman of her neighbour, jewels of silver, and jewels of gold. 3And the LORD gave the people favour in the sight of the Egyptians. Moreover the man Moses *was* very great in the land of Egypt, in the sight of Pharaoh's servants, and in the sight of the people. 4And Moses said, Thus saith the LORD, About _____ will I go out into the midst of Egypt: 5And all the _____ in the land of Egypt shall _____, from the firstborn of _____ that sitteth upon his throne, even unto the firstborn of the _____ that *is* behind the mill; and all the firstborn of _____. 6And there shall be a great _____ throughout all the land of Egypt, such as there was none like it, nor shall be like it any more. 7But against any of the children of Israel shall not a dog move his tongue, against man or beast: that ye may know how that the LORD doth put a _____ between the Egyptians and Israel. 8And all these thy servants shall come down unto me, and bow down themselves unto me, saying, Get thee out, and all the people that follow thee: and after that I will go out. And he went out from Pharaoh in a great _____. 9And the LORD said unto Moses, Pharaoh shall not hearken unto you; that my wonders may be multiplied in the land of Egypt. 10And Moses and Aaron did all these wonders before Pharaoh: and the LORD hardened Pharaoh's heart, so that he would not let the children of Israel go out of his land.

12:1And the LORD spake unto Moses and Aaron in the land of Egypt, saying, 2This month *shall be* unto you the beginning of months: it *shall be* the _____ month of the year to you.

3Speak ye unto all the congregation of Israel, saying, In the _____ *day* of this month they shall take to them every man a _____, according to the house of *their* fathers, _____ lamb for an house: 4And if the household be too little for the lamb, let him and his _____ next unto his house take *it* according to the number of the souls; every man according to his eating shall make your count for _____ _____. 5_____ lamb shall be without _____, a _____ of the _____ year: ye shall take *it* out from the sheep, or from the goats: 6And ye shall _____ it up until the _____ day of the same month: and the whole assembly of the congregation of Israel shall _____ it in the _____. 7And they shall take of the _____, and _____ *it* on the _____ side _____ and on the _____ door _____ of the houses, wherein they shall eat it. 8And they shall eat the flesh in that night, _____ with fire, and _____ bread; *and* with bitter *herbs* they shall eat it. 9Eat _____ of it raw, nor sodden at all with water, but roast *with* fire; his head with his legs, and with the purtenance thereof. 10And ye shall let _____ of it remain until the morning; and that which remaineth of it until the morning ye shall _____ with fire.

11And thus shall ye _____ it; *with* your loins _____, your _____ on your feet, and your _____ in your _____; and ye shall eat it in _____: it *is* the LORD'S _____. 12For I will pass through the land of Egypt this night, and will smite all the firstborn in the land of Egypt, both man and beast; and against all the _____ of Egypt I will execute judgment: I *am* the LORD. 13And the _____ shall be to you for a _____ upon the houses where ye *are:* and when I

_____ the blood, I will _____ over you, and the plague shall not be upon you to destroy *you,* when I smite the land of Egypt. ¹⁴And this day shall be unto you for a memorial; and ye shall keep it a feast to the Lord throughout your generations; ye shall keep it a feast by an ordinance for ever. ¹⁵Seven days shall ye eat _____ bread; even the first day ye shall _____ away leaven out of your _____: for whosoever eateth leavened bread from the first day until the seventh day, that soul shall be cut off from Israel. ¹⁶And in the first day *there shall be* an holy convocation, and in the seventh day there shall be an holy convocation to you; no manner of _____ shall be done in them, save *that* which every man must eat, that only may be done of you. ¹⁷And ye shall observe *the feast of* unleavened bread; for in this selfsame day have I brought your armies out of the land of Egypt: therefore shall ye observe this day in your generations by an ordinance for ever.

¹⁸In the first *month,* on the fourteenth day of the month at even, ye shall eat unleavened bread, until the one and twentieth day of the month at even. ¹⁹Seven days shall there be no _____ found in your houses: for whosoever eateth that which is leavened, even that soul shall be cut off from the congregation of Israel, whether he be a stranger, or born in the land. ²⁰Ye shall eat nothing leavened; in all your habitations shall ye eat unleavened bread.

²¹Then Moses called for all the elders of Israel, and said unto them, Draw out and take you a lamb according to your families, and _____ the passover. ²²And ye shall take a bunch of hyssop, and dip *it* in the blood that *is* in the bason, and strike the _____ and the two side _____ with the blood that *is* in the bason; and none of you shall go out at the door of his house until the morning. ²³For the Lord will pass through to smite the Egyptians; and when he seeth the _____ upon the lintel, and on the two side posts, the Lord will _____ over the door, and will _____ suffer the _____ to come in unto your houses to smite *you.* ²⁴And ye shall observe this thing for an ordinance to thee and to thy sons for ever. ²⁵And it shall come to pass, when ye be come to the land which the Lord will give you, according as he hath promised, that ye shall keep this service. ²⁶And it shall come to pass, when your children shall say unto you, What mean ye by this service? ²⁷That ye shall say, It *is* the _____ of the _____ passover, who passed over the houses of the children of Israel in Egypt, when he smote the Egyptians, and delivered our houses. And the people bowed the head and _____. ²⁸And the children of Israel went away, and _____ as the Lord had commanded Moses and Aaron, so did they.

²⁹And it came to pass, that at _____ the Lord smote all the _____ in the land of Egypt, from the firstborn of Pharaoh that sat on his throne unto the firstborn of the captive that *was* in the dungeon; and all the firstborn of cattle. ³⁰And Pharaoh rose up in the night, he, and all his servants, and all the Egyptians; and there was a great cry in Egypt; for *there was* not a house where *there was* not one dead.

³¹And he called for Moses and Aaron by night, and said, Rise up, *and* get you forth from among my people, both ye and the children of Israel; and go, serve the Lord, as ye have said. ³²Also take your flocks and your herds, as ye have said, and be _____; and _____ me also. ³³And the Egyptians were urgent upon the people, that they might send them out of the land in haste; for they said, We *be* all dead *men.* ³⁴And the people took their dough before it was leavened, their kneadingtroughs being bound up in their clothes upon their shoulders. ³⁵And the children of Israel did according to the word

of Moses; and they borrowed of the Egyptians jewels of silver, and jewels of gold, and raiment: ³⁶And the LORD gave the people favour in the sight of the Egyptians, so that they lent unto them *such things as they required.* And they _____ the Egyptians.

³⁷And the children of Israel journeyed from Rameses to Succoth, about _____ hundred _____ on foot *that were* men, beside children. ³⁸And a mixed multitude went up also with them; and flocks, and herds, *even* very much cattle. ³⁹And they baked unleavened cakes of the dough which they brought forth out of Egypt, for it was not leavened; because they were thrust out of Egypt, and could not tarry, neither had they prepared for themselves any victual.

⁴⁰Now the sojourning of the children of Israel, who dwelt in Egypt, *was* _____ hundred and _____ years. ⁴¹And it came to pass at the end of the four hundred and thirty years, even the selfsame day it came to pass, that all the hosts of the LORD went out from the land of Egypt. ⁴²It *is* a night to be much _____ unto the LORD for bringing them out from the land of Egypt: this *is* that night of the LORD to be observed of all the children of Israel in their generations.

⁴³And the LORD said unto Moses and Aaron, This *is* the ordinance of the passover: There shall no stranger eat thereof: ⁴⁴But every man's servant that is bought for money, when thou hast circumcised him, then shall he eat thereof. ⁴⁵A foreigner and an hired servant shall not eat thereof. ⁴⁶In one house shall it be eaten; thou shalt not carry forth ought of the flesh abroad out of the house; neither shall ye _____ a _____ thereof. ⁴⁷All the congregation of Israel shall keep it. ⁴⁸And when a stranger shall sojourn with thee, and will keep the passover to the LORD, let all his males be circumcised, and then let him come near and keep it; and he shall be as one that is born in the land: for no uncircumcised person shall eat thereof. ⁴⁹One law shall be to him that is homeborn, and unto the stranger that sojourneth among you. ⁵⁰Thus did all the children of Israel; as the LORD commanded Moses and Aaron, so did they. ⁵¹And it came to pass the selfsame day, *that* the LORD did bring the children of Israel out of the land of Egypt by their armies.

^{13:1}And the LORD spake unto Moses, saying, ²_____ unto me all the firstborn, whatsoever openeth the womb among the children of Israel, *both* of man and of beast: it *is* mine.

³And Moses said unto the people, _____ this day, in which ye came out from Egypt, out of the house of bondage; for by strength of hand the LORD brought you out from this *place:* there shall no leavened bread be eaten. ⁴This day came ye out in the month _____.

⁵And it shall be when the LORD shall bring thee into the land of the Canaanites, and the Hittites, and the Amorites, and the Hivites, and the Jebusites, which he sware unto thy fathers to give thee, a land _____ with _____ and _____, that thou shalt keep this service in this month. ⁶Seven days thou shalt eat unleavened bread, and in the seventh day *shall be* a feast to the LORD. ⁷Unleavened bread shall be eaten seven days; and there shall no leavened bread be seen with thee, neither shall there be leaven seen with thee in all thy quarters.

⁸And thou shalt shew thy son in that day, saying, *This is done* because of that *which* the LORD did unto me when I came forth out of Egypt. ⁹And it shall be for a sign unto thee upon thine hand, and for a memorial between thine eyes, that the LORD'S law may be in

thy mouth: for with a strong hand hath the _____ brought thee _____ of Egypt. ¹⁰Thou shalt therefore keep this ordinance in his season from year to year.

¹¹And it shall be when the _____ shall bring thee _____ the land of the Canaanites, as he sware unto thee and to thy fathers, and shall give it thee, ¹²That thou shalt set apart unto the LORD all that openeth the matrix, and every firstling that cometh of a beast which thou hast; the males *shall be* the LORD'S. ¹³And every firstling of an ass thou shalt redeem with a lamb; and if thou wilt not redeem it, then thou shalt _____ his _____ : and all the firstborn of man among thy children shalt thou redeem.

¹⁴And it shall be when thy son asketh thee in time to come, saying, What *is* this? that thou shalt say unto him, By strength of hand the LORD brought us out from Egypt, from the house of bondage: ¹⁵And it came to pass, when Pharaoh would hardly let us go, that the LORD slew all the firstborn in the land of Egypt, both the firstborn of man, and the firstborn of beast: therefore I sacrifice to the LORD all that openeth the matrix, being males; but all the firstborn of my children I redeem. ¹⁶And it shall be for a token upon thine hand, and for frontlets between thine eyes: for by strength of hand the LORD brought us forth out of Egypt.

¹⁷And it came to pass, when Pharaoh had let the people go, that God led them _____ *through* the way of the land of the Philistines, although that *was* near; for God said, Lest peradventure the people repent when they see war, and they return to Egypt: ¹⁸But God led the people about, *through* the way of the _____ of the Red sea: and the children of Israel went up harnessed out of the land of Egypt. ¹⁹And Moses took the _____ of Joseph with him: for he had straitly sworn the children of Israel, saying, God will surely visit you; and ye shall carry up my bones away hence with you.

²⁰And they took their journey from Succoth, and encamped in Etham, in the edge of the wilderness. ²¹And the LORD went before them by day in a pillar of a _____ , to lead them the way; and by night in a pillar of _____ , to give them light; to go by day and night: ²²He took not away the pillar of the cloud by day, nor the pillar of fire by night, *from* before the people.

¹⁴:¹And the LORD spake unto Moses, saying, ²Speak unto the children of Israel, that they turn and encamp before Pi-hahiroth, between Migdol and the sea, over against Baal-zephon: before it shall ye encamp by the sea. ³For Pharaoh will say of the children of Israel, They *are* entangled in the land, the wilderness hath shut them in. ⁴And I will harden Pharaoh's heart, that he shall _____ after them; and I will be _____ upon Pharaoh, and upon all his host; that the Egyptians may know that I *am* the LORD. And they did so.

⁵And it was told the king of Egypt that the people fled: and the heart of Pharaoh and of his servants was turned against the people, and they said, _____ have we done this, that we have let Israel go from _____ us? ⁶And he made ready his chariot, and took his people with him: ⁷And he took _____ hundred chosen chariots, and all the chariots of Egypt, and captains over every one of them. ⁸And the LORD hardened the heart of Pharaoh king of Egypt, and he pursued after the children of Israel: and the children of Israel went out with an high hand. ⁹But the Egyptians pursued after them, all the horses *and* chariots of Pharaoh, and his horsemen, and his army, and overtook them encamping by the sea, beside Pi-hahiroth, before Baal-zephon.

¹⁰And when Pharaoh drew nigh, the children of Israel lifted up their eyes, and, behold, the Egyptians marched after them; and they were sore _____: and the children of Israel _____ out unto the LORD. ¹¹And they said unto Moses, Because *there were* no graves in Egypt, hast thou taken us away to die in the wilderness? wherefore hast thou dealt thus with us, to carry us forth out of Egypt? ¹²*Is* not this the word that we did tell thee in Egypt, saying, Let us alone, that we may serve the Egyptians? For *it had been* better for us to serve the Egyptians, than that we should die in the wilderness.

¹³And Moses said unto the people, _____ ye _____, _____ _____, and see the _____ of the LORD, which he will shew to you to day: for the Egyptians whom ye have seen to day, ye shall see them again no more for _____. ¹⁴The _____ shall _____ for you, and _____ shall _____ your _____.

¹⁵And the LORD said unto Moses, Wherefore criest thou unto me? speak unto the children of Israel, that they go _____: ¹⁶But lift thou up thy _____, and stretch out thine hand over the sea, and _____ it: and the children of Israel shall go on _____ *ground* through the _____ of the sea. ¹⁷And I, behold, I will harden the hearts of the Egyptians, and they shall follow them: and I will get me honour upon Pharaoh, and upon all his host, upon his chariots, and upon his horsemen. ¹⁸And the Egyptians shall know that I *am* the LORD, when I have gotten me honour upon Pharaoh, upon his chariots, and upon his horsemen.

¹⁹And the _____ of God, which went before the camp of Israel, removed and went _____ them; and the pillar of the cloud went from before their face, and stood _____ them: ²⁰And it came between the camp of the Egyptians and the camp of Israel; and it was a cloud and darkness *to them,* but it gave light by night *to these:* so that the one came not near the other all the night. ²¹And Moses stretched out his hand over the sea; and the LORD caused the sea to go *back* by a strong _____ wind all that night, and made the sea _____ *land,* and the _____ were divided. ²²And the children of Israel went into the midst of the sea upon the _____ *ground:* and the waters *were* a _____ unto them on their right hand, and on their left.

²³And the Egyptians pursued, and went in after them to the midst of the sea, *even* all Pharaoh's horses, his chariots, and his horsemen. ²⁴And it came to pass, that in the morning watch the LORD _____ unto the host of the Egyptians through the pillar of fire and of the cloud, and _____ the host of the Egyptians, ²⁵And took off their chariot _____, that they drave them heavily: so that the Egyptians said, Let us flee from the face of Israel; for the LORD _____ for them against the Egyptians.

²⁶And the LORD said unto Moses, Stretch out thine hand over the sea, that the waters may come again upon the Egyptians, upon their chariots, and upon their horsemen. ²⁷And Moses stretched forth his hand over the sea, and the sea returned to his strength when the morning appeared; and the Egyptians fled against it; and the LORD _____ the Egyptians in the midst of the sea. ²⁸And the waters returned, and covered the chariots, and the horsemen, *and* all the host of Pharaoh that came into the sea after them; there remained not so much as _____ of them. ²⁹But the children of Israel walked upon dry *land* in the midst of the sea; and the waters *were* a wall unto them on their right hand, and on their left. ³⁰Thus the LORD _____ Israel that day out of the hand of the Egyptians; and Israel saw the Egyptians dead upon the sea shore. ³¹And Israel saw that

great work which the LORD did upon the Egyptians: and the people _____ the LORD, and _____ the _____, and his servant _____.

15:1Then _____ Moses and the children of Israel this song unto the LORD, and spake, saying, I will _____ unto the LORD, for he hath _____ gloriously: the horse and his rider hath he thrown into the sea. 2The LORD *is* my _____ and song, and he is become my _____: he *is* my _____, and I will prepare him an habitation; my father's God, and I will _____ him. 3The LORD *is* a man of war: the LORD *is* his name. 4Pharaoh's chariots and his host hath he cast into the sea: his chosen captains also are _____ in the Red sea. 5The depths have covered them: they sank into the bottom as a stone. 6Thy right hand, O LORD, is become glorious in power: thy right hand, O LORD, hath dashed in pieces the enemy. 7And in the greatness of thine excellency thou hast overthrown them that rose up against thee: thou sentest forth thy wrath, *which* consumed them as stubble. 8And with the blast of thy nostrils the waters were gathered together, the floods stood upright as an heap, *and* the depths were congealed in the heart of the sea. 9The enemy said, I will pursue, I will overtake, I will divide the spoil; my lust shall be satisfied upon them; I will draw my sword, my hand shall destroy them. 10Thou didst blow with thy wind, the sea covered them: they sank as lead in the mighty waters. 11Who *is* _____ unto thee, O LORD, among the gods? who *is* _____ thee, glorious in _____, fearful *in* _____, doing _____? 12Thou stretchedst out thy right hand, the earth swallowed them. 13Thou in thy _____ hast led forth the people *which* thou hast redeemed: thou hast guided *them* in thy strength unto thy holy habitation. 14The people shall hear, *and* be afraid: sorrow shall take hold on the inhabitants of Palestina. 15Then the dukes of Edom shall be amazed; the mighty men of Moab, trembling shall take hold upon them; all the inhabitants of Canaan shall melt away. 16Fear and dread shall fall upon them; by the greatness of thine arm they shall be *as* still as a stone; till thy people pass over, O LORD, till the people pass over, *which* thou hast purchased. 17Thou shalt bring them in, and plant them in the mountain of thine inheritance, *in* the place, O LORD, *which* thou hast made for thee to dwell in, in the Sanctuary, O Lord, *which* thy hands have established. 18The LORD shall _____ for ever and ever. 19For the horse of Pharaoh went in with his chariots and with his horsemen into the sea, and the LORD brought again the waters of the sea upon them; but the children of Israel went on dry *land* in the midst of the sea.

20And _____ the _____, the _____ of _____, took a _____ in her hand; and all the _____ went out after her with timbrels and with _____. 21And Miriam answered them, _____ ye to the LORD, for he hath _____ gloriously; the horse and his rider hath he thrown into the sea. 22So Moses brought Israel from the Red sea, and they went out into the wilderness of Shur; and they went three days in the wilderness, and found no _____.

23And when they came to _____, they could not drink of the waters of Marah, for they *were* _____: therefore the name of it was called Marah. 24And the people _____ against Moses, saying, What shall we drink? 25And he cried unto the LORD; and the LORD shewed him a _____, *which* when he had cast into the waters, the waters were made _____: there he made for them a statute and an ordinance, and there he proved them, 26And said, If thou wilt _____ hearken to the _____ of the LORD thy God, and wilt _____ that which is _____ in his sight, and wilt give _____ to his commandments, and _____ all his statutes, I will put

_____ of these diseases upon thee, which I have brought upon the Egyptians: for I *am* the LORD that _____ thee.

²⁷And they came to Elim, where *were* twelve wells of water, and threescore and ten palm trees: and they encamped there by the waters.

¹⁶:¹And they took their journey from Elim, and all the congregation of the children of Israel came unto the wilderness of Sin, which *is* between Elim and Sinai, on the fifteenth day of the second month after their departing out of the land of Egypt. ²And the whole congregation of the children of Israel _____ against Moses and Aaron in the wilderness: ³And the children of Israel said unto them, Would to God we had died by the hand of the LORD in the land of Egypt, when we sat by the flesh pots, *and* when we did eat bread to the full; for ye have brought us forth into this wilderness, to kill this whole assembly with hunger.

⁴Then said the LORD unto Moses, Behold, I will rain _____ from _____ for you; and the people shall go out and gather a certain rate every day, that I may prove them, whether they will walk in my _____, or no. ⁵And it shall come to pass, that on the sixth day they shall prepare *that* which they bring in; and it shall be twice as much as they gather daily. ⁶And Moses and Aaron said unto all the children of Israel, At even, then ye shall know that the LORD hath brought you _____ from the land of Egypt: ⁷And in the morning, then ye shall see the _____ of the LORD; for that he heareth your murmurings against the LORD: and what *are* we, that ye murmur against us? ⁸And Moses said, *This shall be,* when the LORD shall give you in the evening flesh to eat, and in the morning bread to the full; for that the LORD heareth your murmurings which ye murmur against him: and what *are* we? your murmurings *are* not against _____, but against the _____.

⁹And Moses spake unto Aaron, Say unto all the congregation of the children of Israel, Come near before the LORD: for he hath heard your _____. ¹⁰And it came to pass, as Aaron spake unto the whole _____ of the children of Israel, that they looked toward the wilderness, and, behold, the glory of the LORD appeared in the cloud.

¹¹And the LORD spake unto Moses, saying, ¹²I have heard the murmurings of the children of Israel: speak unto them, saying, At even ye shall eat flesh, and in the morning ye shall be filled with bread; and ye shall know that I *am* the LORD your God. ¹³And it came to pass, that at even the _____ came up, and covered the camp: and in the morning the dew lay round about the host. ¹⁴And when the dew that lay was gone up, behold, upon the face of the wilderness *there lay* a small round thing, *as* small as the hoar frost on the ground. ¹⁵And when the children of Israel saw *it,* they said one to another, It *is* _____: for they wist not what it *was.* And Moses said unto them, This *is* the _____ which the LORD hath given you to eat.

¹⁶This *is* the thing which the LORD hath commanded, Gather of it every man *according to* his eating, an omer for every man, according to the number of your persons; take ye every man for *them* which *are* in his tents. ¹⁷And the children of Israel did so, and gathered, some more, some less. ¹⁸And when they did mete *it* with an omer, he that gathered much had nothing over, and he that gathered little had no lack; they gathered every man according to his eating. ¹⁹And Moses said, Let no man leave of it till the morning. ²⁰Notwithstanding they hearkened not unto Moses; but some of them left of it until the morning, and it bred _____, and _____: and Moses was wroth with

them. ²¹And they gathered it every morning, every man according to his eating: and when the sun waxed hot, it melted.

²²And it came to pass, *that* on the _____ day they gathered _____ as much bread, two omers for one *man:* and all the rulers of the congregation came and told Moses. ²³And he said unto them, This *is that* which the LORD hath said, To morrow *is* the rest of the holy _____ unto the LORD: bake *that* which ye will bake *to day,* and seethe that ye will seethe; and that which remaineth over lay up for you to be kept until the morning. ²⁴And they laid it up till the morning, as Moses bade: and it did _____ stink, neither was there any worm therein. ²⁵And Moses said, Eat that to day; for to day *is* a sabbath unto the LORD: to day ye shall not find it in the field. ²⁶Six days ye shall gather it; but on the _____ day, *which is* the sabbath, in it there shall be _____.

²⁷And it came to pass, *that* there went out *some* of the people on the seventh day for to gather, and they found none. ²⁸And the LORD said unto Moses, How long _____ ye to keep my _____ and my laws? ²⁹See, for that the LORD hath given you the sabbath, therefore he giveth you on the sixth day the bread of two days; abide ye every man in his place, let no man go out of his place on the seventh day. ³⁰So the people _____ on the seventh day. ³¹And the house of Israel called the name thereof _____: and it *was* like coriander seed, white; and the taste of it *was* like wafers *made* with _____.

³²And Moses said, This *is* the thing which the LORD commandeth, Fill an omer of it to be kept for your generations; that they may see the bread wherewith I have fed you in the wilderness, when I brought you forth from the land of Egypt. ³³And Moses said unto Aaron, Take a pot, and put an omer full of manna therein, and lay it up before the LORD, to be kept for your generations. ³⁴As the LORD commanded Moses, so Aaron laid it up before the Testimony, to be kept. ³⁵And the children of Israel did eat manna _____ years, until they came to a land inhabited; they did eat manna, until they came unto the borders of the land of Canaan. ³⁶Now an omer *is* the tenth *part* of an ephah.

¹⁷:¹And all the congregation of the children of Israel journeyed from the wilderness of Sin, after their journeys, according to the commandment of the LORD, and pitched in Rephidim: and *there was* no _____ for the people to drink. ²Wherefore the people did _____ with _____, and said, Give us water that we may drink. And Moses said unto them, Why chide ye with _____? wherefore do ye _____ the _____? ³And the people thirsted there for water; and the people _____ against Moses, and said, Wherefore *is* this *that* thou hast brought us up out of Egypt, to kill us and our children and our cattle with _____? ⁴And Moses cried unto the LORD, saying, What shall I do unto this people? they be almost ready to stone me. ⁵And the LORD said unto Moses, Go on before the people, and take with thee of the elders of Israel; and thy _____, wherewith thou smotest the river, take in thine hand, and go. ⁶Behold, I will stand before thee there upon the _____ in Horeb; and thou shalt _____ the rock, and there shall come _____ out of it, that the people may drink. And Moses did so in the sight of the elders of Israel. ⁷And he called the name of the place Massah, and Meribah, because of the chiding of the children of Israel, and because they tempted the LORD, saying, Is the LORD among us, or not?

EXODUS

⁸Then came _____, and _____ with Israel in Rephidim. ⁹And Moses said unto _____, Choose us out men, and go out, fight with Amalek: to morrow I will stand on the top of the hill with the rod of God in mine hand. ¹⁰So Joshua did as Moses had said to him, and fought with Amalek: and Moses, _____, and _____ went up to the top of the hill. ¹¹And it came to pass, when Moses held _____ his _____, that Israel _____: and when he let _____ his hand, Amalek _____. ¹²But Moses' hands *were* _____; and they took a _____, and put *it* under him, and he sat thereon; and Aaron and Hur _____ up his hands, the one on the one side, and the other on the other side; and his hands were _____ until the going down of the sun. ¹³And Joshua discomfited Amalek and his people with the edge of the sword. ¹⁴And the LORD said unto Moses, Write this *for* a memorial in a book, and rehearse *it* in the ears of Joshua: for I will utterly put out the remembrance of Amalek from under heaven. ¹⁵And Moses built an altar, and called the name of it _____-_____: ¹⁶For he said, Because the LORD hath sworn *that* the LORD *will have* war with Amalek from generation to generation.

^{18:1}When Jethro, the priest of Midian, Moses' father in law, heard of all that God had done for Moses, and for Israel his people, *and* that the LORD had brought Israel out of Egypt; ²Then Jethro, Moses' father in law, took _____, Moses' _____, after he had sent her back, ³And her two sons; of which the name of the one *was* _____; for he said, I have been an alien in a strange land: ⁴And the name of the other *was* _____; for the God of my father, *said he, was* mine help, and delivered me from the sword of Pharaoh: ⁵And Jethro, Moses' father in law, came with his sons and his wife unto Moses into the wilderness, where he encamped at the mount of God: ⁶And he said unto Moses, I thy father in law Jethro am come unto thee, and thy wife, and her two sons with her.

⁷And Moses went out to meet his father in law, and did obeisance, and kissed him; and they asked each other of *their* welfare; and they came into the tent. ⁸And Moses told his father in law all that the LORD had done unto Pharaoh and to the Egyptians for Israel's sake, *and* all the travail that had come upon them by the way, and *how* the LORD delivered them. ⁹And Jethro rejoiced for all the goodness which the LORD had done to Israel, whom he had delivered out of the hand of the Egyptians. ¹⁰And Jethro said, Blessed *be* the LORD, who hath delivered you out of the hand of the Egyptians, and out of the hand of Pharaoh, who hath delivered the people from under the hand of the Egyptians. ¹¹Now I know that the _____ *is* _____ than all _____: for in the thing wherein they dealt proudly *he was* _____ them. ¹²And Jethro, Moses' father in law, took a burnt offering and sacrifices for God: and Aaron came, and all the elders of Israel, to eat bread with Moses' father in law before God.

¹³And it came to pass on the morrow, that Moses sat to _____ the people: and the people stood by Moses from the morning unto the evening. ¹⁴And when Moses' father in law saw all that he did to the people, he said, What *is* this thing that thou doest to the people? why sittest thou thyself _____, and all the people stand by thee from morning unto even? ¹⁵And Moses said unto his father in law, Because the people come unto me to enquire of God: ¹⁶When they have a matter, they come unto me; and I judge between one and another, and I do make *them* know the statutes of God, and his laws. ¹⁷And Moses' father in law said unto him, The thing that thou doest *is* not good. ¹⁸Thou wilt surely _____ away, both thou, and this people that *is* with thee: for this thing *is*

too _____ for thee; thou art not able to perform it thyself _____. [19]Hearken now unto my voice, I will give thee counsel, and God shall be with thee: Be thou for the people to God-ward, that thou mayest bring the causes unto God: [20]And thou shalt teach them ordinances and laws, and shalt shew them the way wherein they _____ walk, and the work that they must do. [21]Moreover thou shalt provide out of all the people able men, such as _____ God, men of _____, hating _____; and place *such* over them, *to be* rulers of thousands, *and* rulers of hundreds, rulers of fifties, and rulers of tens: [22]And let them judge the people at all seasons: and it shall be, *that* every great matter they shall bring unto thee, but every small matter they shall judge: so shall it be easier for thyself, and they shall _____ *the* _____ with thee. [23]If thou shalt do this thing, and God command thee *so,* then thou shalt be able to endure, and all this people shall also go to their place in peace. [24]So Moses hearkened to the voice of his father in law, and did all that he had said. [25]And Moses chose able men out of all Israel, and made them heads over the people, rulers of thousands, rulers of hundreds, rulers of fifties, and rulers of tens. [26]And they judged the people at all seasons: the hard causes they brought unto Moses, but every small matter they judged themselves.

[27]And Moses let his father in law depart; and he went his way into his own land.

[19:1]In the third month, when the children of Israel were gone forth out of the land of Egypt, the same day came they *into* the wilderness of _____. [2]For they were departed from Rephidim, and were come *to* the desert of Sinai, and had pitched in the wilderness; and there Israel camped before the mount. [3]And Moses went up unto God, and the LORD called unto him out of the mountain, saying, Thus shalt thou say to the house of Jacob, and tell the children of Israel; [4]Ye have seen what I did unto the Egyptians, and *how* I bare you on eagles' wings, and brought you unto myself. [5]Now therefore, if ye will _____ my voice indeed, and keep my covenant, then ye shall be a peculiar treasure unto me above all people: for all the earth *is* mine: [6]And ye shall be unto me a kingdom of priests, and an holy nation. These *are* the words which thou shalt speak unto the children of Israel.

[7]And Moses came and called for the elders of the people, and laid before their faces all these words which the LORD commanded him. [8]And all the people answered together, and said, _____ that the LORD hath _____ we will do. And Moses returned the words of the people unto the LORD. [9]And the LORD said unto Moses, Lo, I come unto thee in a thick cloud, that the people may hear when I speak with _____, and believe _____ for _____. And Moses told the words of the people unto the LORD.

[10]And the LORD said unto Moses, Go unto the people, and _____ them to day and to morrow, and let them wash their clothes, [11]And be ready against the third day: for the third day the LORD will come down in the sight of all the people upon mount Sinai. [12]And thou shalt set bounds unto the people round about, saying, Take heed to yourselves, *that ye* go *not* up into the mount, or touch the border of it: whosoever toucheth the mount shall be surely put to _____: [13]There shall not an hand touch it, but he shall surely be stoned, or shot through; whether *it be* beast or man, it shall not live: when the trumpet soundeth long, they shall come up to the mount.

[14]And Moses went down from the mount unto the people, and sanctified the people; and they washed their clothes. [15]And he said unto the people, Be ready against the third day: come not at *your* wives.

¹⁶And it came to pass on the third day in the morning, that there were thunders and lightnings, and a thick cloud upon the mount, and the voice of the trumpet exceeding loud; so that all the _____ that *was* in the camp _____. ¹⁷And Moses brought forth the people out of the camp to meet with God; and they stood at the nether part of the mount. ¹⁸And mount Sinai was altogether on a _____, because the LORD descended upon it in _____: and the smoke thereof ascended as the smoke of a furnace, and the whole mount quaked greatly. ¹⁹And when the voice of the trumpet sounded long, and waxed louder and louder, Moses spake, and _____ answered him by a _____. ²⁰And the LORD came down upon mount Sinai, on the top of the mount: and the LORD called Moses *up* to the top of the mount; and Moses went up. ²¹And the LORD said unto Moses, Go down, charge the people, lest they break through unto the LORD to gaze, and many of them perish. ²²And let the priests also, which come near to the LORD, sanctify themselves, lest the LORD break forth upon them. ²³And Moses said unto the LORD, The people cannot come up to mount Sinai: for thou chargedst us, saying, Set bounds about the mount, and sanctify it. ²⁴And the LORD said unto him, Away, get thee down, and thou shalt come up, thou, and Aaron with thee: but let not the priests and the people break through to come up unto the LORD, lest he break forth upon them. ²⁵So Moses went down unto the people, and spake unto them.

²⁰:¹And God spake all these words, saying, ²I *am* the LORD thy God, which have brought thee out of the land of Egypt, out of the house of bondage. ³Thou shalt have no _____ _____ before me. ⁴Thou shalt not make unto thee any _____ _____, or any likeness *of any thing* that *is* in heaven above, or that *is* in the earth beneath, or that *is* in the water under the earth: ⁵Thou shalt not bow _____ thyself to them, nor _____ them: for I the LORD thy God *am* a _____ God, visiting the iniquity of the fathers upon the children unto the third and fourth *generation* of them that hate me; ⁶And shewing mercy unto _____ of them that love me, and keep my commandments. ⁷Thou shalt not take the _____ of the LORD thy God in vain; for the LORD will not hold him guiltless that taketh his name in vain. ⁸_____ the sabbath day, to keep it _____. ⁹Six days shalt thou _____, and do all thy work: ¹⁰But the _____ day *is* the _____ of the _____ thy God: *in it* thou shalt not do any _____, thou, nor thy son, nor thy daughter, thy manservant, nor thy maidservant, nor thy cattle, nor thy stranger that *is* within thy gates: ¹¹For *in* six days the LORD made heaven and earth, the sea, and all that in them *is,* and rested the seventh day: wherefore the LORD _____ the sabbath day, and hallowed it.

¹²_____ thy father and thy mother: that thy days may be long upon the land which the LORD thy God giveth thee. ¹³Thou shalt not _____. ¹⁴Thou shalt not commit _____. ¹⁵Thou shalt not _____. ¹⁶Thou shalt not bear _____ witness against thy neighbour. ¹⁷Thou shalt not _____ thy neighbour's house, thou shalt not covet thy neighbour's wife, nor his manservant, nor his maidservant, nor his ox, nor his ass, nor _____ thing that *is* thy neighbour's.

¹⁸And all the people saw the thunderings, and the lightnings, and the noise of the trumpet, and the mountain smoking: and when the people saw *it,* they removed, and stood afar off. ¹⁹And they said unto Moses, Speak thou with us, and we will hear: but let not God speak with us, lest we die. ²⁰And Moses said unto the people, _____ not: for God is come to _____ you, and that his fear may be before your faces, that ye

_____not. ²¹And the people stood afar off, and Moses drew near unto the thick darkness where God *was.*

²²And the L ORD said unto Moses, Thus thou shalt say unto the children of Israel, Ye have seen that I have talked with you from heaven. ²³Ye shall not _____with me _____of silver, neither shall ye make unto you _____of gold.

²⁴An _____of earth thou shalt make unto me, and shalt sacrifice thereon thy burnt offerings, and thy peace offerings, thy sheep, and thine oxen: in all places where I record my name I will come unto thee, and I will bless thee. ²⁵And if thou wilt make me an altar of stone, thou shalt _____build it of _____stone: for if thou lift up thy _____upon it, thou hast _____it. ²⁶Neither shalt thou go up by steps unto mine altar, that thy _____be not discovered thereon.

²¹:¹Now these *are* the judgments which thou shalt set before them. ²If thou buy an Hebrew servant, _____years he shall serve: and in the seventh he shall go out _____for nothing. ³If he came in by himself, he shall go out by himself: if he were married, then his wife shall go out with him. ⁴If his master have given him a wife, and she have born him sons or daughters; the wife and her children shall be her master's, and he shall go out by himself. ⁵And if the servant shall plainly say, I love my master, my wife, and my children; I will not go out free: ⁶Then his master shall bring him unto the judges; he shall also bring him to the door, or unto the door post; and his master shall bore his _____through with an _____; and he shall serve him for _____.

⁷And if a man sell his daughter to be a maidservant, she shall _____go out as the menservants do. ⁸If she please not her master, who hath betrothed her to himself, then shall he let her be redeemed: to sell her unto a strange nation he shall have no power, seeing he hath dealt deceitfully with her. ⁹And if he have betrothed her unto his son, he shall deal with her after the manner of daughters. ¹⁰If he take him another *wife;* her food, her raiment, and her duty of marriage, shall he not diminish. ¹¹And if he do not these three unto her, then shall she go out free without money.

¹²He that smiteth a man, so that he _____, shall be surely put to _____. ¹³And if a man lie _____in wait, but God deliver *him* into his hand; then I will appoint thee a _____whither he shall _____. ¹⁴But if a man come _____upon his neighbour, to slay him with _____; thou shalt take him from mine altar, that he may _____.

¹⁵And he that smiteth his _____, or his _____, shall be surely put to _____.

¹⁶And he that _____a man, and _____him, or if he be found in his hand, he shall surely be put to _____.

¹⁷And he that _____his _____, or his _____, shall surely be put to _____.

¹⁸And if men strive together, and one smite another with a stone, or with *his* fist, and he die not, but keepeth *his* bed: ¹⁹If he rise again, and walk abroad upon his staff, then shall he that smote *him* be quit: only he shall _____*for* the _____of his time, and shall cause *him* to be thoroughly healed.

²⁰And if a man smite his servant, or his maid, with a rod, and he die under his hand; he shall be surely _____. ²¹Notwithstanding, if he continue a day or two, he shall not be punished: for he *is* his money.

²²If men strive, and hurt a woman with child, so that her fruit depart *from her,* and yet no mischief follow: he shall be surely _____, according as the woman's husband will lay upon him; and he shall pay as the judges *determine.* ²³And if *any* mischief follow, then thou shalt give _____ for _____, ²⁴ _____ for _____, _____ for _____, _____ for _____, _____ for _____, ²⁵ _____ for _____, _____ for _____, _____ for _____.

²⁶And if a man smite the eye of his servant, or the eye of his maid, that it perish; he shall let him go _____ for his eye's sake. ²⁷And if he smite out his manservant's tooth, or his maidservant's tooth; he shall let him go _____ for his tooth's sake.

²⁸If an ox gore a man or a woman, that they die: then the ox shall be surely stoned, and his flesh shall not be eaten; but the owner of the ox *shall be* quit. ²⁹But if the ox were wont to push with his horn in time past, and it hath been _____ to his owner, and he hath not kept him in, but that he hath killed a man or a woman; the ox shall be stoned, and his _____ also shall be put to _____. ³⁰If there be laid on him a sum of money, then he shall give for the _____ of his life whatsoever is laid upon him. ³¹Whether he have gored a son, or have gored a daughter, according to this judgment shall it be done unto him. ³²If the ox shall push a manservant or a maidservant; he shall give unto their master thirty shekels of silver, and the ox shall be stoned.

³³And if a man shall open a pit, or if a man shall dig a pit, and not cover it, and an ox or an ass fall therein; ³⁴The owner of the pit shall make *it* _____, *and* give _____ unto the owner of them; and the dead *beast* shall be his.

³⁵And if one man's ox hurt another's, that he die; then they shall sell the live ox, and divide the money of it; and the dead *ox* also they shall divide. ³⁶Or if it be known that the ox hath used to push in time past, and his owner hath not kept him in; he shall surely pay ox for ox; and the dead shall be his own.

²²:¹If a man shall steal an ox, or a sheep, and kill it, or sell it; he shall _____ five oxen for an ox, and four sheep for a sheep.

²If a _____ be found breaking up, and be smitten that he die, *there shall* no blood *be shed* for him. ³If the sun be risen upon him, *there shall be* blood *shed* for him; *for* he should make full _____; if he have nothing, then he shall be sold for his theft. ⁴If the theft be certainly found in his hand alive, whether it be ox, or ass, or sheep; he shall restore _____.

⁵If a man shall cause a field or vineyard to be eaten, and shall put in his beast, and shall feed in another man's field; of the best of his own field, and of the best of his own vineyard, shall he make _____.

⁶If fire break out, and catch in thorns, so that the stacks of corn, or the standing corn, or the field, be consumed *therewith;* he that kindled the fire shall surely make _____.

⁷If a man shall deliver unto his neighbour money or stuff to keep, and it be stolen out of the man's house; if the thief be found, let him pay _____. ⁸If the thief be not found, then the master of the house shall be brought unto the judges, *to see* whether he have put his hand unto his neighbour's goods. ⁹For all manner of trespass, *whether it be* for ox, for ass, for sheep, for raiment, *or* for any manner of lost thing, which *another* challengeth to be his, the cause of both parties shall come before the judges; *and* whom the judges shall condemn, he shall pay double unto his neighbour. ¹⁰If a man deliver unto his neighbour an ass, or an ox, or a sheep, or any beast, to keep; and it die, or be hurt, or driven away,

no man seeing *it:* ¹¹*Then* shall an oath of the LORD be between them both, that he hath not put his hand unto his neighbour's goods; and the owner of it shall accept *thereof,* and he shall not make *it* good. ¹²And if it be _____ from him, he shall make _____ unto the owner thereof. ¹³If it be _____ in pieces, *then* let him bring it *for* witness, *and* he shall not make good that which was torn.

¹⁴And if a man _____ *ought* of his neighbour, and it be _____, or _____, the owner thereof *being* _____ with it, he shall surely _____ *it* _____. ¹⁵*But* if the owner thereof *be* _____ it, he shall _____ make *it* good: if it *be* an _____ *thing,* it came for his _____.

¹⁶And if a man _____ a maid that is not betrothed, and lie with her, he shall surely endow her to be his _____. ¹⁷If her father utterly _____ to give her unto him, he shall _____ money according to the dowry of virgins.

¹⁸Thou shalt not suffer a _____ to live.

¹⁹Whosoever lieth with a _____ shall surely be put to _____.

²⁰He that _____ unto *any* _____, save unto the LORD only, he shall be utterly _____.

²¹Thou shalt neither vex a _____, nor oppress him: for ye were strangers in the land of Egypt.

²²Ye shall not afflict any _____, or _____ child. ²³If thou afflict them in any wise, and they _____ at all unto me, I will surely _____ their cry; ²⁴And my _____ shall wax hot, and I will _____ you with the sword; and your wives shall be _____, and your children _____.

²⁵If thou _____ money to *any of* my people *that is* poor by thee, thou shalt not be to him as an _____, neither shalt thou lay upon him _____. ²⁶If thou at all take thy neighbour's raiment to pledge, thou shalt deliver it unto him by that the sun goeth down: ²⁷For that *is* his covering only, it *is* his raiment for his skin: wherein shall he sleep? and it shall come to pass, when he crieth unto me, that I will hear; for I *am* _____.

²⁸Thou shalt not revile the _____, nor curse the _____ of thy people.

²⁹Thou shalt not delay *to offer* the _____ of thy ripe fruits, and of thy liquors: the _____ of thy sons shalt thou give unto me. ³⁰Likewise shalt thou do with thine oxen, *and* with thy sheep: seven days it shall be with his dam; on the eighth day thou shalt give it me.

³¹And ye shall be _____ men unto me: neither shall ye eat *any* flesh *that is* torn of _____ in the field; ye shall cast it to the dogs.

²³:¹Thou shalt not raise a _____ report: put not thine hand with the wicked to be an _____ witness.

²Thou shalt not follow a multitude to *do* _____; neither shalt thou speak in a cause to decline after many to wrest *judgment:*

³Neither shalt thou countenance a poor man in his cause.

⁴If thou meet thine enemy's ox or his ass going astray, thou shalt surely bring it back to him again. ⁵If thou see the ass of him that hateth thee lying under his burden, and wouldest forbear to help him, thou shalt surely help with him. ⁶Thou shalt not wrest the judgment of thy poor in his cause. ⁷Keep thee _____ from a false matter; and the innocent and righteous slay thou not: for I will not justify the wicked.

⁸And thou shalt take no _____: for the gift _____ the wise, and _____ the words of the righteous.

⁹Also thou shalt not oppress a stranger: for ye know the heart of a stranger, seeing ye were strangers in the land of Egypt. ¹⁰And six years thou shalt _____ thy land, and shalt gather in the fruits thereof: ¹¹But the _____ *year* thou shalt let it _____ and lie still; that the poor of thy people may eat: and what they leave the beasts of the field shall eat. In like manner thou shalt deal with thy vineyard, *and* with thy oliveyard. ¹²Six days thou shalt do thy work, and on the seventh day thou shalt rest: that thine ox and thine ass may rest, and the son of thy handmaid, and the stranger, may be _____. ¹³And in all *things* that I have said unto you be _____: and make no _____ of the _____ of other gods, neither let it be _____ out of thy _____.

¹⁴Three times thou shalt keep a feast unto me in the year. ¹⁵Thou shalt keep the feast of _____ _____: (thou shalt eat unleavened bread seven days, as I commanded thee, in the time appointed of the month Abib; for in it thou camest out from Egypt: and none shall appear before me empty:) ¹⁶And the feast of _____, the firstfruits of thy labours, which thou hast sown in the field: and the feast of _____, *which is* in the end of the year, when thou hast gathered in thy labours out of the field. ¹⁷Three times in the year all thy males shall appear before the Lord GOD. ¹⁸Thou shalt not offer the blood of my sacrifice with leavened bread; neither shall the fat of my sacrifice remain until the morning. ¹⁹The first of the firstfruits of thy land thou shalt bring into the house of the LORD thy God. Thou shalt not seethe a kid in his mother's milk.

²⁰Behold, I send an _____ before thee, to keep thee in the way, and to bring thee into the place which I have prepared. ²¹_____ of him, and _____ his voice, provoke him _____; for he will not _____ your transgressions: for my name *is* in him. ²²But if thou shalt indeed _____ his voice, and do all that I speak; then I will be an enemy unto thine enemies, and an adversary unto thine adversaries. ²³For mine Angel shall go before thee, and bring thee in unto the Amorites, and the Hittites, and the Perizzites, and the Canaanites, and the Hivites, and the Jebusites: and I will cut them off. ²⁴Thou shalt _____ _____ down to their gods, nor serve them, nor do after their _____: but thou shalt utterly overthrow them, and quite _____ down their _____. ²⁵And ye shall _____ the LORD your God, and he shall _____ thy bread, and thy water; and I will take _____ _____ from the midst of thee.

²⁶There shall nothing cast their young, nor be barren, in thy land: the number of thy days I will fulfil. ²⁷I will send my fear before thee, and will destroy all the people to whom thou shalt come, and I will make all thine enemies turn their backs unto thee. ²⁸And I will send _____ before thee, which shall drive out the Hivite, the Canaanite, and the Hittite, from before thee. ²⁹I will _____ drive them out from before thee in _____ _____; lest the land become desolate, and the beast of the field multiply against thee. ³⁰By _____ and _____ I will drive them out from before thee, until thou be increased, and inherit the land. ³¹And I will set thy bounds from the _____ _____ even unto the _____ of the _____, and from the desert unto the river: for I will deliver the inhabitants of the land into your hand; and thou shalt drive them out before thee. ³²Thou shalt make no covenant with them, nor with their gods. ³³They shall not dwell in thy land, lest they make thee _____ against me: for if thou serve their gods, it will surely be a _____ unto thee.

EXODUS

^{24:1}And he said unto Moses, Come up unto the LORD, thou, and Aaron, Nadab, and Abihu, and seventy of the elders of Israel; and worship ye afar off. ²And Moses alone shall come near the LORD: but they shall not come nigh; neither shall the people go up with him.

³And Moses came and told the people all the words of the LORD, and all the judgments: and all the people answered with one voice, and said, All the words which the LORD hath said will we do. ⁴And Moses wrote all the words of the LORD, and rose up early in the morning, and builded an altar under the hill, and twelve pillars, according to the twelve tribes of Israel. ⁵And he sent young men of the children of Israel, which offered burnt offerings, and sacrificed peace offerings of oxen unto the LORD. ⁶And Moses took half of the blood, and put *it* in basons; and half of the blood he sprinkled on the altar. ⁷And he took the book of the covenant, and read in the audience of the people: and they said, All that the LORD hath said will we do, and be obedient. ⁸And Moses took the blood, and sprinkled *it* on the people, and said, Behold the blood of the covenant, which the LORD hath made with you concerning all these words.

⁹Then went up Moses, and Aaron, Nadab, and Abihu, and seventy of the elders of Israel: ¹⁰And they _____ the God of Israel: and *there was* under his feet as it were a paved work of a sapphire stone, and as it were the body of heaven in *his* clearness. ¹¹And upon the nobles of the children of Israel he laid not his hand: also they saw God, and did eat and drink.

¹²And the LORD said unto Moses, Come up to me into the mount, and be there: and I will give thee tables of _____, and a _____, and _____which I have written; that thou mayest teach them. ¹³And Moses rose up, and his _____ _____: and Moses went up into the mount of God. ¹⁴And he said unto the elders, Tarry ye here for us, until we come again unto you: and, behold, Aaron and Hur *are* with you: if any man have any matters to do, let him come unto them. ¹⁵And Moses went up into the mount, and a cloud covered the mount. ¹⁶And the glory of the LORD abode upon mount Sinai, and the cloud covered it six days: and the seventh day he called unto Moses out of the midst of the cloud. ¹⁷And the sight of the glory of the LORD *was* like devouring fire on the top of the mount in the eyes of the children of Israel. ¹⁸And Moses went into the midst of the cloud, and gat him up into the mount: and Moses was in the mount _____days and _____nights.

^{25:1}And the LORD spake unto Moses, saying, ²Speak unto the children of Israel, that they bring me an offering: of every man that _____ it _____with his _____ye shall take my offering. ³And this *is* the offering which ye shall take of them; gold, and silver, and brass, ⁴And blue, and purple, and scarlet, and fine linen, and goats' *hair,* ⁵And rams' skins dyed red, and badgers' skins, and shittim wood, ⁶Oil for the light, spices for _____oil, and for sweet _____, ⁷Onyx stones, and stones to be set in the _____, and in the _____. ⁸And let them make me a _____; that I may dwell among them. ⁹According to all that I shew thee, *after* the pattern of the tabernacle, and the pattern of all the instruments thereof, even so shall ye make *it.*

¹⁰And they shall make an _____*of* shittim wood: two cubits and a half *shall be* the length thereof, and a cubit and a half the breadth thereof, and a cubit and a half the height thereof. ¹¹And thou shalt overlay it with pure _____, within and without shalt thou overlay it, and shalt make upon it a crown of gold round about. ¹²And thou shalt cast four rings of gold for it, and put *them* in the four corners thereof; and two rings

shall be in the one side of it, and two rings in the other side of it. ¹³And thou shalt make staves *of* shittim wood, and overlay them with gold. ¹⁴And thou shalt put the staves into the rings by the sides of the ark, that the ark may be borne with them. ¹⁵The staves shall be in the rings of the ark: they shall not be taken from it. ¹⁶And thou shalt put _____ the ark the testimony which I shall give thee. ¹⁷And thou shalt make a mercy seat *of* pure gold: two cubits and a half *shall be* the length thereof, and a cubit and a half the breadth thereof. ¹⁸And thou shalt make two cherubims *of* gold, *of* beaten work shalt thou make them, in the two ends of the _____ seat. ¹⁹And make one cherub on the one end, and the other cherub on the other end: *even* of the mercy seat shall ye make the cherubims on the two ends thereof. ²⁰And the cherubim shall stretch forth *their* wings on high, _____ the mercy seat with their wings, and their faces *shall look* one to another; toward the mercy seat shall the faces of the cherubims be. ²¹And thou shalt put the mercy seat above upon the ark; and in the ark thou shalt put the testimony that I shall give thee. ²²And there I will meet with thee, and I will _____ with thee from _____ the mercy seat, from between the two cherubims which *are* upon the ark of the testimony, of all *things* which I will give thee in commandment unto the children of Israel.

²³Thou shalt also make a _____ *of* shittim wood: two cubits *shall be* the length thereof, and a cubit the breadth thereof, and a cubit and a half the height thereof. ²⁴And thou shalt overlay it with pure gold, and make thereto a crown of gold round about. ²⁵And thou shalt make unto it a border of an hand breadth round about, and thou shalt make a golden crown to the border thereof round about. ²⁶And thou shalt make for it four rings of gold, and put the rings in the four corners that *are* on the four feet thereof. ²⁷Over against the border shall the rings be for places of the staves to bear the table. ²⁸And thou shalt make the staves *of* shittim wood, and overlay them with gold, that the table may be borne with them. ²⁹And thou shalt make the dishes thereof, and spoons thereof, and covers thereof, and bowls thereof, to cover withal: *of* pure gold shalt thou make them. ³⁰And thou shalt set upon the table _____ before me alway.

³¹And thou shalt make a _____ *of* pure gold: *of* beaten work shall the candlestick be made: his shaft, and his branches, his bowls, his knops, and his flowers, shall be of the same. ³²And _____ branches shall come out of the sides of it; three branches of the candlestick out of the one side, and three branches of the candlestick out of the other side: ³³Three bowls made like unto almonds, *with* a knop and a flower in one branch; and three bowls made like almonds in the other branch, *with* a knop and a flower: so in the six branches that come out of the candlestick. ³⁴And in the candlestick *shall be* four bowls made like unto almonds, *with* their knops and their flowers. ³⁵And *there shall be* a knop under two branches of the same, and a knop under two branches of the same, and a knop under two branches of the same, according to the six branches that proceed out of the candlestick. ³⁶Their knops and their branches shall be of the same: all it *shall be* one beaten work *of* pure gold. ³⁷And thou shalt make the _____ lamps thereof: and they shall light the lamps thereof, that they may give light over against it. ³⁸And the tongs thereof, and the snuffdishes thereof, *shall be of* pure gold. ³⁹*Of* a talent of pure gold shall he make it, with all these vessels. ⁴⁰And look that thou make *them* after their _____, which was _____ thee in the _____.

²⁶:¹Moreover thou shalt make the tabernacle *with* ten curtains *of* fine twined linen, and blue, and purple, and scarlet: *with* cherubims of cunning work shalt thou make them.

²The length of one curtain *shall be* eight and twenty cubits, and the breadth of one curtain four cubits: and every one of the curtains shall have one measure. ³The five curtains shall be coupled together one to another; and *other* five curtains *shall be* coupled one to another. ⁴And thou shalt make loops of blue upon the edge of the one curtain from the selvedge in the coupling; and likewise shalt thou make in the uttermost edge of *another* curtain, in the coupling of the second. ⁵Fifty loops shalt thou make in the one curtain, and fifty loops shalt thou make in the edge of the curtain that is in the coupling of the second; that the loops may take hold one of another. ⁶And thou shalt make fifty taches of gold, and couple the curtains together with the taches: and it shall be one tabernacle.

⁷And thou shalt make curtains *of* goats' *hair* to be a covering upon the tabernacle: eleven curtains shalt thou make. ⁸The length of one curtain *shall be* thirty cubits, and the breadth of one curtain four cubits: and the eleven curtains *shall be all* of one measure. ⁹And thou shalt couple five curtains by themselves, and six curtains by themselves, and shalt double the sixth curtain in the forefront of the tabernacle. ¹⁰And thou shalt make fifty loops on the edge of the one curtain *that is* outmost in the coupling, and fifty loops in the edge of the curtain which coupleth the second. ¹¹And thou shalt make fifty taches of brass, and put the taches into the loops, and couple the tent together, that it may be one. ¹²And the remnant that remaineth of the curtains of the tent, the half curtain that remaineth, shall hang over the backside of the tabernacle. ¹³And a cubit on the one side, and a cubit on the other side of that which remaineth in the length of the curtains of the tent, it shall hang over the sides of the tabernacle on this side and on that side, to cover it. ¹⁴And thou shalt make a covering for the tent *of* rams' skins dyed red, and a covering above *of* badgers' skins.

¹⁵And thou shalt make boards for the tabernacle *of* shittim wood standing up. ¹⁶Ten cubits *shall be* the length of a board, and a cubit and a half *shall be* the breadth of one board. ¹⁷Two tenons *shall there be* in one board, set in order one against another: thus shalt thou make for all the boards of the tabernacle. ¹⁸And thou shalt make the boards for the tabernacle, twenty boards on the south side southward. ¹⁹And thou shalt make forty sockets of silver under the twenty boards; two sockets under one board for his two tenons, and two sockets under another board for his two tenons. ²⁰And for the second side of the tabernacle on the north side *there shall be* twenty boards: ²¹And their forty sockets *of* silver; two sockets under one board, and two sockets under another board. ²²And for the sides of the tabernacle westward thou shalt make six boards. ²³And two boards shalt thou make for the corners of the tabernacle in the two sides. ²⁴And they shall be coupled together beneath, and they shall be coupled together above the head of it unto one ring: thus shall it be for them both; they shall be for the two corners. ²⁵And they shall be eight boards, and their sockets *of* silver, sixteen sockets; two sockets under one board, and two sockets under another board.

²⁶And thou shalt make bars *of* shittim wood; five for the boards of the one side of the tabernacle, ²⁷And five bars for the boards of the other side of the tabernacle, and five bars for the boards of the side of the tabernacle, for the two sides westward. ²⁸And the middle bar in the midst of the boards shall reach from end to end. ²⁹And thou shalt overlay the boards with gold, and make their rings *of* gold *for* places for the bars: and thou shalt overlay the bars with gold. ³⁰And thou shalt rear up the tabernacle according to the fashion thereof which was shewed thee in the mount.

³¹And thou shalt make a _____ *of* blue, and purple, and scarlet, and fine twined linen of cunning work: with cherubims shall it be made: ³²And thou shalt hang it upon four pillars of shittim *wood* overlaid with gold: their hooks *shall be of* gold, upon the four sockets of silver.

³³And thou shalt hang up the _____ under the taches, that thou mayest bring in thither _____ the _____ the _____ of the _____: and the _____ shall _____ unto you between the _____ *place* and the _____ _____. ³⁴And thou shalt put the _____ seat _____ the _____ of the testimony in the _____ _____ *place.* ³⁵And thou shalt set the _____ _____ the vail, and the _____ over against the table on the _____ of the tabernacle toward the _____: and thou shalt put the _____ on the _____ side. ³⁶And thou shalt make an hanging for the door of the tent, *of* blue, and purple, and scarlet, and fine twined linen, wrought with needlework. ³⁷And thou shalt make for the hanging five pillars *of* shittim *wood,* and overlay them with gold, *and* their hooks *shall be of* gold: and thou shalt cast five sockets of brass for them.

^{27:1}And thou shalt make an _____ *of* shittim wood, five cubits long, and five cubits broad; the altar shall be foursquare: and the height thereof *shall be* three cubits. ²And thou shalt make the _____ of it upon the _____ corners thereof: his horns shall be of the same: and thou shalt overlay it with _____. ³And thou shalt make his pans to receive his ashes, and his shovels, and his basons, and his fleshhooks, and his firepans: all the vessels thereof thou shalt make *of* _____. ⁴And thou shalt make for it a grate of network *of* brass; and upon the net shalt thou make four brasen rings in the four corners thereof. ⁵And thou shalt put it under the compass of the altar beneath, that the net may be even to the midst of the altar. ⁶And thou shalt make staves for the altar, staves *of* shittim wood, and overlay them with brass. ⁷And the staves shall be put into the rings, and the staves shall be upon the two sides of the altar, to bear it. ⁸Hollow with boards shalt thou make it: as it was shewed thee in the mount, so shall they make *it.*

⁹And thou shalt make the court of the tabernacle: for the south side southward *there shall be* hangings for the court *of* fine twined linen of an hundred cubits long for one side: ¹⁰And the twenty pillars thereof and their twenty sockets *shall be of* brass; the hooks of the pillars and their fillets *shall be of* silver. ¹¹And likewise for the north side in length *there shall be* hangings of an hundred *cubits* long, and his twenty pillars and their twenty sockets *of* brass; the hooks of the pillars and their fillets *of* silver.

¹²And *for* the breadth of the court on the west side *shall be* hangings of fifty cubits: their pillars ten, and their sockets ten. ¹³And the breadth of the court on the east side eastward *shall be* fifty cubits. ¹⁴The hangings of one side *of the gate shall be* fifteen cubits: their pillars three, and their sockets three. ¹⁵And on the other side *shall be* hangings fifteen *cubits:* their pillars three, and their sockets three.

¹⁶And for the gate of the court *shall be* an hanging of twenty cubits, *of* blue, and purple, and scarlet, and fine twined linen, wrought with needlework: *and* their pillars *shall be* four, and their sockets four. ¹⁷All the pillars round about the court *shall be* filleted with silver; their hooks *shall be of* silver, and their sockets of brass.

¹⁸The length of the court *shall be* an hundred cubits, and the breadth fifty every where, and the height five cubits *of* fine twined linen, and their sockets *of* brass. ¹⁹All the vessels

of the tabernacle in all the service thereof, and all the pins thereof, and all the pins of the court, *shall be of* brass.

²⁰And thou shalt command the children of Israel, that they bring thee pure _____olive beaten for the _____, to cause the lamp to burn _____. ²¹In the tabernacle of the congregation without the vail, which *is* before the testimony, Aaron and his sons shall order it from evening to morning before the LORD: *it shall be* a statute for ever unto their generations on the behalf of the children of Israel.

^{28:1}And take thou unto thee Aaron thy brother, and his sons with him, from among the children of Israel, that he may minister unto me in the priest's office, *even* Aaron, Nadab and Abihu, Eleazar and Ithamar, Aaron's sons. ²And thou shalt make _____ _____for Aaron thy brother for glory and for beauty. ³And thou shalt speak unto all *that are* wise hearted, whom I have filled with the spirit of wisdom, that they may make Aaron's garments to _____ _____, that he may _____unto me in the priest's office. ⁴And these *are* the garments which they shall make; a _____, and an _____, and a _____, and a broidered _____, a _____, and a _____: and they shall make holy garments for Aaron thy brother, and his sons, that he may minister unto me in the priest's office. ⁵And they shall take gold, and blue, and purple, and scarlet, and fine linen.

⁶And they shall make the ephod *of* gold, *of* blue, and *of* purple, *of* scarlet, and fine twined linen, with cunning work. ⁷It shall have the two shoulderpieces thereof joined at the two edges thereof; and *so* it shall be joined together. ⁸And the curious girdle of the ephod, which *is* upon it, shall be of the same, according to the work thereof; *even of* gold, *of* blue, and purple, and scarlet, and fine twined linen. ⁹And thou shalt take two onyx stones, and grave on them the names of the children of Israel: ¹⁰Six of their names on one stone, and *the other* six names of the rest on the other stone, according to their birth. ¹¹With the work of an engraver in stone, *like* the engravings of a signet, shalt thou engrave the two stones with the names of the children of Israel: thou shalt make them to be set in ouches of gold. ¹²And thou shalt _____the two stones upon the _____of the ephod *for* stones of memorial unto the children of Israel: and Aaron shall _____their names _____the LORD upon his two shoulders for a memorial.

¹³And thou shalt make ouches *of* gold; ¹⁴And two chains *of* pure gold at the ends; *of* wreathen work shalt thou make them, and fasten the wreathen chains to the ouches.

¹⁵And thou shalt make the breastplate of judgment with cunning work; after the work of the ephod thou shalt make it; *of* gold, *of* blue, and *of* purple, and *of* scarlet, and *of* fine twined linen, shalt thou make it. ¹⁶Foursquare it shall be *being* doubled; a span *shall be* the length thereof, and a span *shall be* the breadth thereof. ¹⁷And thou shalt set in it settings of stones, *even* four rows of stones: *the first* row *shall be* a _____, a _____, and a _____: *this shall be* the first row. ¹⁸And the second row *shall be* an _____, a _____, and a _____. ¹⁹And the third row a _____, an _____, and an _____. ²⁰And the fourth row a _____, and an _____, and a _____: they shall be set in gold in their inclosings. ²¹And the stones shall be with the names of the children of Israel, twelve, according to their names, *like* the engravings of a signet; every one with his name shall they be according to the twelve tribes.

²²And thou shalt make upon the breastplate chains at the ends *of* wreathen work *of* pure gold. ²³And thou shalt make upon the breastplate two rings of gold, and shalt put the two rings on the two ends of the breastplate. ²⁴And thou shalt put the two wreathen *chains* of gold in the two rings *which are* on the ends of the breastplate. ²⁵And *the other* two ends of the two wreathen *chains* thou shalt fasten in the two ouches, and put *them* on the shoulderpieces of the ephod before it.

²⁶And thou shalt make two rings of gold, and thou shalt put them upon the two ends of the breastplate in the border thereof, which *is* in the side of the ephod inward. ²⁷And two *other* rings of gold thou shalt make, and shalt put them on the two sides of the ephod underneath, toward the forepart thereof, over against the *other* coupling thereof, above the curious girdle of the ephod. ²⁸And they shall bind the breastplate by the rings thereof unto the rings of the ephod with a lace of blue, that *it* may be above the curious girdle of the ephod, and that the breastplate be not loosed from the ephod. ²⁹And Aaron shall _____ the names of the children of Israel in the _____ of judgment _____ his _____, when he goeth in unto the holy *place,* for a memorial before the Lord continually.

³⁰And thou shalt put in the breastplate of judgment the _____ and the _____; and they shall be _____ Aaron's _____, when he goeth in before the Lord: and Aaron shall _____ the judgment of the children of Israel upon his _____ before the Lord _____.

³¹And thou shalt make the robe of the ephod all *of* blue. ³²And there shall be an hole in the top of it, in the midst thereof: it shall have a binding of woven work round about the hole of it, as it were the hole of an habergeon, that it be not rent.

³³And *beneath* upon the hem of it thou shalt make pomegranates *of* blue, and *of* purple, and *of* scarlet, round about the hem thereof; and bells of gold between them round about: ³⁴A golden bell and a pomegranate, a golden bell and a pomegranate, upon the hem of the robe round about. ³⁵And it shall be upon Aaron to minister: and his sound shall be heard when he goeth in unto the holy *place* before the Lord, and when he cometh out, that he die not.

³⁶And thou shalt make a plate *of* pure gold, and grave upon it, *like* the engravings of a signet, _____ TO THE _____. ³⁷And thou shalt put it on a blue lace, that it may be upon the mitre; upon the forefront of the mitre it shall be. ³⁸And it shall be upon Aaron's forehead, that Aaron may bear the iniquity of the holy things, which the children of Israel shall hallow in all their holy gifts; and it shall be always upon his forehead, that they may be accepted before the Lord.

³⁹And thou shalt embroider the coat of fine linen, and thou shalt make the mitre *of* fine linen, and thou shalt make the girdle *of* needlework.

⁴⁰And for Aaron's sons thou shalt make coats, and thou shalt make for them girdles, and bonnets shalt thou make for them, for glory and for beauty. ⁴¹And thou shalt put them upon Aaron thy brother, and his sons with him; and shalt _____ them, and _____ them, and _____ them, that they may _____ unto me in the priest's _____. ⁴²And thou shalt make them linen _____ to cover their _____; from the _____ even unto the _____ they shall reach: ⁴³And they shall be upon Aaron, and upon his sons, when they come in unto the tabernacle of the congregation, or when they come near unto the altar to minister in the holy *place;* that

they bear not iniquity, and die: *it shall be* a statute for ever unto him and his seed after him.

²⁹:¹And this *is* the thing that thou shalt do unto them to hallow them, to minister unto me in the priest's office: Take one young bullock, and two rams without blemish, ²And unleavened bread, and cakes unleavened tempered with oil, and wafers unleavened anointed with oil: *of* wheaten flour shalt thou make them. ³And thou shalt put them into one basket, and bring them in the basket, with the bullock and the two rams. ⁴And Aaron and his sons thou shalt bring unto the door of the tabernacle of the congregation, and shalt wash them with water. ⁵And thou shalt take the garments, and put upon Aaron the coat, and the robe of the ephod, and the ephod, and the breastplate, and gird him with the curious girdle of the ephod: ⁶And thou shalt put the mitre upon his head, and put the holy crown upon the mitre. ⁷Then shalt thou take the anointing oil, and pour *it* upon his head, and anoint him. ⁸And thou shalt bring his sons, and put coats upon them. ⁹And thou shalt gird them with girdles, Aaron and his sons, and put the bonnets on them: and the priest's office shall be theirs for a perpetual statute: and thou shalt consecrate Aaron and his sons. ¹⁰And thou shalt cause a bullock to be brought before the tabernacle of the congregation: and Aaron and his sons shall put their hands upon the head of the bullock. ¹¹And thou shalt kill the bullock before the LORD, *by* the door of the tabernacle of the congregation. ¹²And thou shalt take of the blood of the bullock, and put *it* upon the horns of the altar with thy finger, and pour all the blood beside the bottom of the altar. ¹³And thou shalt take all the fat that covereth the inwards, and the caul *that is* above the liver, and the two kidneys, and the fat that is upon them, and burn *them* upon the altar. ¹⁴But the flesh of the bullock, and his skin, and his dung, shalt thou burn with fire without the camp: it *is* a _____ offering.

¹⁵Thou shalt also take one ram; and Aaron and his sons shall put their hands upon the head of the ram. ¹⁶And thou shalt slay the ram, and thou shalt take his blood, and sprinkle *it* round about upon the altar. ¹⁷And thou shalt cut the ram in pieces, and wash the inwards of him, and his legs, and put *them* unto his pieces, and unto his head. ¹⁸And thou shalt burn the whole ram upon the altar: it *is* a burnt offering unto the LORD: it *is* a _____ _____, an offering made by fire unto the LORD.

¹⁹And thou shalt take the other ram; and Aaron and his sons shall put their hands upon the head of the ram. ²⁰Then shalt thou kill the ram, and take of his blood, and put *it* upon the tip of the right _____ of Aaron, and upon the tip of the right _____ of his sons, and upon the _____ of their right hand, and upon the great _____ of their right foot, and sprinkle the blood upon the altar round about. ²¹And thou shalt take of the blood that *is* upon the altar, and of the anointing oil, and sprinkle *it* upon Aaron, and upon his garments, and upon his sons, and upon the garments of his sons with him: and he shall be hallowed, and his garments, and his sons, and his sons' garments with him. ²²Also thou shalt take of the ram the fat and the rump, and the fat that covereth the inwards, and the *caul* above the liver, and the two kidneys, and the fat that *is* upon them, and the right shoulder; for it *is* a ram of consecration: ²³And one loaf of bread, and one cake of oiled bread, and one wafer out of the basket of the unleavened bread that *is* before the LORD: ²⁴And thou shalt put all in the hands of Aaron, and in the hands of his sons; and shalt wave them *for* a wave offering before the LORD. ²⁵And thou shalt receive them of their hands, and burn *them* upon the altar for a burnt offering, for a sweet savour before the LORD: it *is* an offering made by fire unto the LORD. ²⁶And thou shalt take the

breast of the ram of Aaron's consecration, and wave it *for* a _____ offering before the LORD: and it shall be thy part. ²⁷And thou shalt sanctify the breast of the wave offering, and the shoulder of the _____ offering, which is waved, and which is heaved up, of the ram of the consecration, *even* of *that* which *is* for Aaron, and of *that* which is for his sons: ²⁸And it shall be Aaron's and his sons' by a statute for ever from the children of Israel: for it *is* an _____ offering: and it shall be an _____ offering from the children of Israel of the sacrifice of their _____ offerings, *even* their heave offering unto the LORD.

²⁹And the holy _____ of Aaron shall be his sons' _____ him, to be anointed therein, and to be consecrated in them. ³⁰*And* that son that is priest in his stead shall put them _____ seven days, when he cometh into the tabernacle of the congregation to minister in the holy *place.*

³¹And thou shalt take the ram of the consecration, and seethe his flesh in the holy place. ³²And Aaron and his sons shall eat the flesh of the ram, and the bread that *is* in the basket, *by* the door of the tabernacle of the congregation. ³³And they shall eat those things wherewith the atonement was made, to consecrate *and* to sanctify them: but a stranger shall not eat *thereof,* because they *are* holy. ³⁴And if ought of the flesh of the consecrations, or of the bread, remain unto the morning, then thou shalt burn the remainder with fire: it shall not be eaten, because it *is* holy. ³⁵And thus shalt thou do unto Aaron, and to his sons, according to all *things* which I have commanded thee: seven days shalt thou consecrate them. ³⁶And thou shalt offer every day a bullock *for* a sin offering for atonement: and thou shalt cleanse the altar, when thou hast made an atonement for it, and thou shalt anoint it, to sanctify it. ³⁷_____ days thou shalt make an atonement for the altar, and sanctify it; and it shall be an altar most holy: _____ _____ the _____ shall be _____ .

³⁸Now this *is that* which thou shalt offer upon the altar; two lambs of the first year day by day _____ . ³⁹The one lamb thou shalt offer in the morning; and the other lamb thou shalt offer at even: ⁴⁰And with the one lamb a tenth deal of flour mingled with the fourth part of an hin of beaten oil; and the fourth part of an hin of wine *for* a drink offering. ⁴¹And the other lamb thou shalt offer at even, and shalt do thereto according to the meat offering of the morning, and according to the drink offering thereof, for a sweet savour, an offering made by fire unto the LORD. ⁴²*This shall be* a _____ burnt offering throughout your generations *at* the door of the tabernacle of the congregation before the LORD: where I will meet you, to speak there unto thee. ⁴³And there I will meet with the children of Israel, and *the tabernacle* shall be sanctified by my glory. ⁴⁴And I will _____ the _____ of the congregation, and the altar: I will sanctify also both Aaron and his sons, to minister to me in the priest's office.

⁴⁵And I will _____ among the children of Israel, and will be their _____ . ⁴⁶And they shall _____ that I *am* the LORD their God, that brought them forth _____ of the land of _____ , that I may _____ among them: I *am* the _____ their _____ .

^{30:1}And thou shalt make an _____ to burn _____ upon: *of* shittim wood shalt thou make it. ²A cubit *shall be* the length thereof, and a cubit the breadth thereof; foursquare shall it be: and two cubits *shall be* the height thereof: the horns thereof *shall be* of the same. ³And thou shalt overlay it with pure gold, the top thereof, and the sides thereof round about, and the horns thereof; and thou shalt make unto it a crown of gold

round about. ⁴And two golden rings shalt thou make to it under the crown of it, by the two corners thereof, upon the two sides of it shalt thou make *it;* and they shall be for places for the staves to bear it withal. ⁵And thou shalt make the staves *of* shittim wood, and overlay them with gold. ⁶And thou shalt put it before the vail that *is* by the ark of the testimony, before the mercy seat that *is* over the testimony, where I will meet with thee. ⁷And Aaron shall burn thereon sweet _____every morning: when he dresseth the lamps, he shall burn incense upon it. ⁸And when Aaron lighteth the lamps at even, he shall burn incense upon it, a _____incense before the LORD throughout your generations. ⁹Ye shall offer no strange incense thereon, nor burnt sacrifice, nor meat offering; neither shall ye pour drink offering thereon. ¹⁰And Aaron shall make an atonement upon the horns of it once in a year with the blood of the sin offering of atonements: once in the year shall he make atonement upon it throughout your generations: it *is* most holy unto the LORD.

¹¹And the LORD spake unto Moses, saying, ¹²When thou takest the sum of the children of Israel after their number, then shall they give every man a ransom for his soul unto the LORD, when thou numberest them; that there be no plague among them, when *thou* numberest them. ¹³This they shall _____, every one that passeth among them that are numbered, half a shekel after the shekel of the sanctuary: (a shekel *is* twenty gerahs:) an half shekel *shall be* the offering of the LORD. ¹⁴Every one that passeth among them that are numbered, from twenty years old and above, shall give an offering unto the LORD. ¹⁵The rich shall not give more, and the poor shall not give less than half a shekel, when *they* give an offering unto the LORD, to make an atonement for your souls. ¹⁶And thou shalt take the atonement money of the children of Israel, and shalt appoint it for the service of the tabernacle of the congregation; that it may be a memorial unto the children of Israel before the LORD, to make an atonement for your souls.

¹⁷And the LORD spake unto Moses, saying, ¹⁸Thou shalt also make a _____*of* brass, and his foot *also of* brass, to wash *withal:* and thou shalt put it between the tabernacle of the congregation and the altar, and thou shalt put water therein. ¹⁹For Aaron and his sons shall _____their hands and their feet thereat: ²⁰When they go into the tabernacle of the congregation, they shall wash with water, that they die not; or when they come near to the altar to minister, to burn offering made by fire unto the LORD: ²¹So they shall wash their hands and their feet, that they die not: and it shall be a statute for ever to them, *even* to him and to his seed throughout their generations.

²²Moreover the LORD spake unto Moses, saying, ²³Take thou also unto thee principal spices, of pure _____five hundred *shekels,* and of sweet _____half so much, *even* two hundred and fifty *shekels,* and of sweet _____two hundred and fifty *shekels,* ²⁴And of _____five hundred *shekels,* after the shekel of the sanctuary, and of _____ _____an hin: ²⁵And thou shalt make it an _____of _____ _____, an ointment compound after the art of the _____: it shall be an holy _____oil. ²⁶And thou shalt anoint the tabernacle of the congregation therewith, and the ark of the testimony, ²⁷And the table and all his vessels, and the candlestick and his vessels, and the altar of incense, ²⁸And the altar of burnt offering with all his vessels, and the laver and his foot. ²⁹And thou shalt sanctify them, that they may be most holy: whatsoever toucheth them shall be holy. ³⁰And thou shalt anoint Aaron and his sons, and consecrate them, that *they* may minister unto me in the priest's office. ³¹And thou shalt speak unto the children of Israel, saying, This shall be an

holy anointing oil unto me throughout your generations. ³²Upon man's flesh shall it not be poured, neither shall ye make *any other* like it, after the composition of it: it *is* _____, *and* it shall be holy unto you. ³³Whosoever compoundeth *any* like it, or whosoever putteth *any* of it upon a stranger, shall even be cut off from his people.

³⁴And the LORD said unto Moses, Take unto thee sweet spices, _____, and _____, and _____; *these* sweet spices with pure _____: of each shall there be a like *weight:* ³⁵And thou shalt make it a _____, a confection after the art of the apothecary, tempered together, pure *and* _____: ³⁶And thou shalt beat *some* of it very small, and put of it before the testimony in the tabernacle of the congregation, where I will meet with thee: it shall be unto you most holy. ³⁷And *as for* the perfume which thou shalt make, ye shall _____ make to _____ according to the composition thereof: it shall be unto thee _____ for the LORD. ³⁸Whosoever shall make like unto that, to _____ thereto, shall even be cut off from his people.

³¹:¹And the LORD spake unto Moses, saying, ²See, I have called by name _____ the son of Uri, the son of Hur, of the tribe of Judah: ³And I have _____ him with the _____ of _____, in _____, and in _____, and in _____, and in all manner of workmanship, ⁴To devise cunning works, to work in gold, and in silver, and in brass, ⁵And in cutting of stones, to set *them,* and in carving of timber, to work in all manner of workmanship. ⁶And I, behold, I have given with him Aholiab, the son of Ahisamach, of the tribe of Dan: and in the hearts of all that are wise hearted I have put wisdom, that they may make all that I have commanded thee; ⁷The tabernacle of the congregation, and the ark of the testimony, and the mercy seat that *is* thereupon, and all the furniture of the tabernacle, ⁸And the table and his furniture, and the pure candlestick with all his furniture, and the altar of incense, ⁹And the altar of burnt offering with all his furniture, and the laver and his foot, ¹⁰And the cloths of service, and the holy garments for Aaron the priest, and the garments of his sons, to minister in the priest's office, ¹¹And the anointing oil, and sweet incense for the holy *place:* according to all that I have commanded thee shall they do.

¹²And the LORD spake unto Moses, saying, ¹³Speak thou also unto the children of Israel, saying, Verily my sabbaths ye shall keep: for it is a _____ between _____ and _____ throughout your generations; that ye may know that I *am* the LORD that doth _____ you. ¹⁴Ye shall keep the sabbath therefore; for it *is* holy unto you: every one that defileth it shall surely be put to death: for whosoever doeth *any* work therein, that soul shall be cut off from among his people. ¹⁵Six days may work be done; but in the seventh is the sabbath of rest, holy to the LORD: whosoever doeth *any* work in the sabbath day, he shall surely be put to death. ¹⁶Wherefore the children of _____ shall keep the sabbath, to _____ the sabbath throughout their generations, *for* a _____ covenant. ¹⁷It *is* a _____ between _____ and the children of _____ for ever: for *in* six days the LORD made heaven and earth, and on the seventh day he rested, and was refreshed.

¹⁸And he gave unto Moses, when he had made an end of communing with him upon mount Sinai, two tables of _____, tables of stone, written with the _____ of God.

³²:¹And when the people saw that Moses delayed to come down out of the mount, the people gathered themselves together unto Aaron, and said unto him, Up, make us gods, which shall go before us; for *as for* this Moses, the man that brought us up out of the land

of Egypt, we wot not what is become of him. ²And Aaron said unto them, Break off the golden earrings, which *are* in the ears of your wives, of your sons, and of your daughters, and bring *them* unto me. ³And all the people brake off the golden earrings which *were* in their ears, and brought *them* unto Aaron. ⁴And he received *them* at their hand, and fashioned it with a graving tool, after he had made it a molten _____: and they said, These *be* thy _____, O Israel, which brought thee up out of the land of Egypt. ⁵And when Aaron saw *it,* he built an _____before it; and Aaron made proclamation, and said, To morrow *is* a feast to the LORD. ⁶And they rose up early on the morrow, and offered burnt offerings, and brought peace offerings; and the people sat down to eat and to drink, and rose up to play.

⁷And the LORD said unto Moses, Go, get thee down; for thy people, which thou broughtest out of the land of Egypt, have _____*themselves:* ⁸They have turned aside quickly out of the way which I commanded them: they have made them a molten calf, and have worshipped it, and have sacrificed thereunto, and said, These *be* thy gods, O Israel, which have brought thee up out of the land of Egypt. ⁹And the LORD said unto Moses, I have seen this people, and, behold, it *is* a _____people: ¹⁰Now therefore let me alone, that my wrath may wax hot against them, and that I may consume them: and I will make of thee a great nation. ¹¹And Moses besought the LORD his God, and said, LORD, why doth thy wrath wax hot against thy people, which thou hast brought forth out of the land of Egypt with great power, and with a mighty hand? ¹²Wherefore should the Egyptians speak, and say, For mischief did he bring them out, to slay them in the mountains, and to consume them from the face of the earth? Turn from thy fierce wrath, and repent of this evil against thy people. ¹³Remember Abraham, Isaac, and Israel, thy servants, to whom thou swarest by thine own self, and saidst unto them, I will multiply your seed as the stars of heaven, and all this land that I have spoken of will I give unto your seed, and they shall inherit *it* for ever. ¹⁴And the LORD repented of the evil which he thought to do unto his people.

¹⁵And Moses turned, and went down from the mount, and the two tables of the testimony *were* in his hand: the tables *were* written on _____their _____; on the one side and on the other *were* they written. ¹⁶And the tables *were* the _____of God, and the writing *was* the _____of God, graven upon the tables. ¹⁷And when Joshua heard the noise of the people as they shouted, he said unto Moses, *There is* a noise of _____in the camp. ¹⁸And he said, *It is* not the voice of *them that* shout for mastery, neither *is it* the voice of *them that* cry for being overcome: *but* the noise of *them that* sing do I hear.

¹⁹And it came to pass, as soon as he came nigh unto the camp, that he saw the calf, and the dancing: and Moses' _____waxed hot, and he cast the tables out of his hands, and brake them beneath the mount. ²⁰And he took the calf which they had made, and _____*it* in the fire, and _____*it* to powder, and strawed *it* upon the _____, and made the children of Israel drink *of it.* ²¹And Moses said unto Aaron, What did this people unto thee, that thou hast brought so great a sin upon them? ²²And Aaron said, Let not the anger of my lord wax hot: thou knowest the people, that they are *set* on mischief. ²³For they said unto me, Make us gods, which shall go before us: for *as for* this Moses, the man that brought us up out of the land of Egypt, we wot not what is become of him. ²⁴And I said unto them, Whosoever hath any gold, let them break *it* off.

So they gave *it* me: then I _____ it into the fire, and there came out this _____.

²⁵And when Moses saw that the people *were* _____; (for Aaron had made them naked unto *their* shame among their enemies:) ²⁶Then Moses stood in the gate of the camp, and said, Who *is* on the LORD'S side? *let him come* unto me. And all the sons of Levi gathered themselves together unto him. ²⁷And he said unto them, Thus saith the LORD God of Israel, Put every man his sword by his side, *and* go in and out from gate to gate throughout the camp, and slay every man his brother, and every man his companion, and every man his neighbour. ²⁸And the children of Levi did according to the word of Moses: and there fell of the people that day about _____ thousand men. ²⁹For Moses had said, Consecrate yourselves to day to the LORD, even every man upon his son, and upon his brother; that he may bestow upon you a blessing this day.

³⁰And it came to pass on the morrow, that Moses said unto the people, Ye have _____ a great sin: and now I will go up unto the LORD; peradventure I shall make an _____ for your sin. ³¹And Moses returned unto the LORD, and said, Oh, this people have sinned a great sin, and have made them gods of gold. ³²Yet now, if thou wilt _____ their sin--; and if not, blot me, I pray thee, out of thy book which thou hast written. ³³And the LORD said unto Moses, Whosoever hath sinned against me, him will I blot out of my book. ³⁴Therefore now go, lead the people unto *the place* of which I have spoken unto thee: behold, mine _____ shall go before thee: nevertheless in the day when I visit I will visit their sin upon them. ³⁵And the LORD _____ the _____, because they made the calf, which Aaron made.

^{33:1}And the LORD said unto Moses, Depart, *and* go up hence, thou and the people which thou hast brought up out of the land of Egypt, unto the land which I sware unto Abraham, to Isaac, and to Jacob, saying, Unto thy seed will I give it: ²And I will send an angel before thee; and I will drive out the Canaanite, the Amorite, and the Hittite, and the Perizzite, the Hivite, and the Jebusite: ³Unto a land flowing with _____ and _____ : for I will not go up in the midst of thee; for thou *art* a stiffnecked people: lest I consume thee in the way.

⁴And when the people heard these evil tidings, they mourned: and no man did put on him his ornaments. ⁵For the LORD had said unto Moses, Say unto the children of Israel, Ye *are* a stiffnecked people: I will come up into the midst of thee in a _____, and consume thee: therefore now put off thy ornaments from thee, that I may know what to do unto thee. ⁶And the children of Israel stripped themselves of their ornaments by the mount Horeb. ⁷And Moses took the tabernacle, and pitched it without the camp, afar off from the camp, and called it the _____ of the _____. And it came to pass, *that* every one which sought the LORD went out unto the tabernacle of the congregation, which *was* _____ the camp. ⁸And it came to pass, when Moses went out unto the tabernacle, *that* all the people rose up, and stood every man *at* his tent door, and looked after Moses, until he was gone into the tabernacle. ⁹And it came to pass, as Moses entered into the tabernacle, the cloudy pillar descended, and stood *at* the door of the tabernacle, and *the* LORD _____ with Moses. ¹⁰And all the people saw the cloudy pillar stand *at* the tabernacle door: and all the people rose up and _____, every man *in* his tent door. ¹¹And the LORD spake unto Moses face to face, as a man speaketh unto his _____. And he turned again into the camp: but his servant _____, the son of Nun, a young man, _____ not _____ of the _____.

¹²And Moses said unto the LORD, See, thou sayest unto me, Bring up this people: and thou hast not let me know _____ thou wilt send _____ me. Yet thou hast said, I know thee by _____, and thou hast also found _____ in my sight. ¹³Now therefore, I pray thee, if I have found grace in thy sight, shew me now _____ way, that I may _____ thee, that I may find grace in thy sight: and consider that this nation *is* thy people. ¹⁴And he said, My _____ shall go *with thee,* and I will give thee _____. ¹⁵And he said unto him, If thy presence go _____ *with me,* carry us _____ up hence. ¹⁶For wherein shall it be known here that I and thy people have found grace in thy sight? *is it* not in that thou goest with us? so shall we be _____, I and thy people, _____ all the _____ that *are* upon the face of the earth. ¹⁷And the LORD said unto Moses, I will do this thing also that thou hast spoken: for thou hast found grace in my sight, and I know thee by name. ¹⁸And he said, I beseech thee, shew me thy _____. ¹⁹And he said, I will make all my _____ pass before thee, and I will proclaim the _____ of the LORD before thee; and will be _____ to whom I will be gracious, and will shew _____ on whom I will shew mercy. ²⁰And he said, Thou canst not see my _____: for there shall no man see me, and _____. ²¹And the LORD said, Behold, *there is* a _____ _____ me, and thou shalt _____ upon a _____: ²²And it shall come to pass, while my glory passeth by, that I will put thee in a _____ of the rock, and will _____ thee with my _____ while I pass by: ²³And I will take away mine hand, and thou shalt see my back parts: but my face shall not be seen.

³⁴:¹And the LORD said unto Moses, Hew thee two tables of stone like unto the first: and I will _____ upon *these* tables the words that were in the first tables, which thou brakest. ²And be ready in the morning, and come up in the morning unto mount Sinai, and present thyself there to me in the top of the mount. ³And no man shall come up with thee, neither let any man be seen throughout all the mount; neither let the flocks nor herds feed before that mount.

⁴And he hewed two tables of stone like unto the first; and Moses rose up early in the morning, and went up unto mount Sinai, as the LORD had commanded him, and took in his hand the two tables of stone. ⁵And the LORD descended in the cloud, and stood with him there, and proclaimed the name of the LORD. ⁶And the LORD passed by before him, and proclaimed, The _____, The _____ God, _____ and _____, _____, and abundant in _____ and _____, ⁷Keeping _____ for thousands, _____ _____ and _____ and _____, and that will by no means _____ *the guilty;* visiting the _____ of the fathers upon the children, and upon the children's children, unto the _____ and to the _____ *generation.* ⁸And Moses made haste, and bowed his head toward the earth, and worshipped. ⁹And he said, If now I have found grace in thy sight, O Lord, let my Lord, I pray thee, go among us; for it *is* a stiffnecked people; and _____ our iniquity and our sin, and take us for thine inheritance.

¹⁰And he said, Behold, I make a _____: before all thy people I will do marvels, such as have not been done in all the earth, nor in any nation: and all the people among which thou *art* shall see the work of the LORD: for it *is* a terrible thing that I will do with thee. ¹¹Observe thou that which I command thee this day: behold, I drive out before thee the Amorite, and the Canaanite, and the Hittite, and the Perizzite, and the Hivite, and the Jebusite. ¹²Take heed to thyself, lest thou make a _____ with the inhabitants of the

land whither thou goest, lest it be for a _____ in the midst of thee: [13]But ye shall destroy their altars, break their images, and cut down their groves: [14]For thou shalt worship no other god: for the LORD, whose name *is* _____, *is* a jealous God: [15]Lest thou make a covenant with the inhabitants of the land, and they go a whoring after their gods, and do sacrifice unto their gods, and *one* call thee, and thou eat of his sacrifice; [16]And thou take of their daughters unto thy sons, and their daughters go a whoring after their gods, and make thy sons go a whoring after their gods. [17]Thou shalt make thee no molten gods.

[18]The feast of _____ _____ shalt thou keep. Seven days thou shalt eat unleavened bread, as I commanded thee, in the time of the month Abib: for in the month Abib thou camest out from Egypt. [19]All that openeth the matrix *is* mine; and every firstling among thy cattle, *whether* ox or sheep, *that is male.* [20]But the firstling of an ass thou shalt redeem with a lamb: and if thou redeem *him* not, then shalt thou break his neck. All the firstborn of thy sons thou shalt redeem. And none shall appear before me empty.

[21]Six days thou shalt work, but on the seventh day thou shalt rest: in earing time and in harvest thou shalt rest.

[22]And thou shalt observe the feast of _____, of the _____ of wheat harvest, and the feast of _____ at the year's end.

[23]_____ in the year shall all your men children appear before the Lord GOD, the God of Israel. [24]For I will cast out the nations before thee, and enlarge thy borders: neither shall any man desire thy land, when thou shalt go up to appear before the LORD thy God thrice in the year. [25]Thou shalt not offer the blood of my sacrifice with leaven; neither shall the sacrifice of the feast of the _____ be left unto the morning. [26]The first of the firstfruits of thy land thou shalt bring unto the house of the LORD thy God. Thou shalt not seethe a kid in his mother's milk. [27]And the LORD said unto Moses, Write thou these words: for after the tenor of these words I have made a covenant with thee and with Israel. [28]And he was there with the LORD _____ days and _____ nights; he did neither _____ bread, nor _____ water. And he wrote upon the tables the words of the covenant, the _____ _____.

[29]And it came to pass, when Moses came down from mount Sinai with the two tables of testimony in Moses' hand, when he came down from the mount, that Moses wist not that the _____ of his face _____ while he talked with him. [30]And when Aaron and all the children of Israel saw Moses, behold, the skin of his face shone; and they were _____ to come nigh him. [31]And Moses called unto them; and Aaron and all the rulers of the congregation returned unto him: and Moses talked with them. [32]And afterward all the children of Israel came nigh: and he gave them in commandment all that the LORD had spoken with him in mount Sinai. [33]And *till* Moses had done speaking with them, he put a _____ on his face. [34]But when Moses went in before the LORD to speak with him, he took the vail off, until he came out. And he came out, and spake unto the children of Israel *that* which he was commanded. [35]And the children of Israel saw the face of Moses, that the skin of Moses' face shone: and Moses put the vail upon his face again, until he went in to speak with him.

[35:1]And Moses gathered all the congregation of the children of Israel together, and said unto them, These *are* the words which the LORD hath commanded, that *ye* should do them. [2]Six days shall work be done, but on the seventh day there shall be to you an holy day, a sabbath of rest to the LORD: whosoever doeth work therein shall be put to death. ³Ye shall kindle no fire throughout your habitations upon the sabbath day.

⁴And Moses spake unto all the congregation of the children of Israel, saying, This *is* the thing which the LORD commanded, saying, ⁵Take ye from among you an offering unto the LORD: whosoever *is* of a _____heart, let him bring it, an _____of the LORD; gold, and silver, and brass, ⁶And blue, and purple, and scarlet, and fine linen, and goats' *hair,* ⁷And rams' skins dyed red, and badgers' skins, and shittim wood, ⁸And oil for the light, and spices for anointing oil, and for the sweet incense, ⁹And onyx stones, and stones to be set for the ephod, and for the breastplate. ¹⁰And every _____hearted among you shall come, and make all that the LORD hath commanded; ¹¹The tabernacle, his tent, and his covering, his taches, and his boards, his bars, his pillars, and his sockets, ¹²The ark, and the staves thereof, *with* the mercy seat, and the vail of the covering, ¹³The table, and his staves, and all his vessels, and the shewbread, ¹⁴The candlestick also for the light, and his furniture, and his lamps, with the oil for the light, ¹⁵And the incense altar, and his staves, and the anointing oil, and the sweet incense, and the hanging for the door at the entering in of the tabernacle, ¹⁶The altar of burnt offering, with his brasen grate, his staves, and all his vessels, the laver and his foot, ¹⁷The hangings of the court, his pillars, and their sockets, and the hanging for the door of the court, ¹⁸The pins of the tabernacle, and the pins of the court, and their cords, ¹⁹The cloths of service, to do service in the holy *place,* the holy garments for Aaron the priest, and the garments of his sons, to minister in the priest's office.

²⁰And all the congregation of the children of Israel departed from the presence of Moses. ²¹And they came, every one whose _____ _____ _____ _____, and every one whom his _____ made _____, *and* they brought the LORD's offering to the _____of the tabernacle of the congregation, and for all his _____, and for the holy _____. ²²And they came, both men and women, as many as were _____hearted, *and* brought bracelets, and earrings, and rings, and tablets, all jewels of gold: and every man that offered *offered* an offering of gold unto the LORD. ²³And every man, with whom was found blue, and purple, and scarlet, and fine linen, and goats' *hair,* and red skins of rams, and badgers' skins, brought *them.* ²⁴Every one that did offer an offering of silver and brass brought the LORD's offering: and every man, with whom was found shittim wood for any work of the service, brought *it.* ²⁵And all the women that were wise _____did spin with their hands, and brought that which they had spun, *both* of blue, and of purple, *and* of scarlet, and of fine linen. ²⁶And all the women whose _____stirred them up in _____spun goats' *hair.* ²⁷And the rulers brought onyx stones, and stones to be set, for the ephod, and for the breastplate; ²⁸And spice, and oil for the light, and for the anointing oil, and for the sweet incense. ²⁹The children of Israel brought a _____ _____unto the LORD, _____man and woman, whose _____made them _____to bring for all manner of work, which the LORD had commanded to be made by the hand of Moses.

³⁰And Moses said unto the children of Israel, See, the LORD hath called by name Bezaleel the son of Uri, the son of Hur, of the tribe of Judah; ³¹And he hath filled him with the spirit of God, in wisdom, in understanding, and in knowledge, and in all manner of workmanship; ³²And to devise curious works, to work in gold, and in silver, and in brass, ³³And in the cutting of stones, to set *them,* and in carving of wood, to make any manner of cunning work. ³⁴And he hath put in his heart that he may teach, *both* he, and

Aholiab, the son of Ahisamach, of the tribe of Dan. ³⁵Them hath he filled with wisdom of heart, to work all manner of work, of the engraver, and of the cunning workman, and of the embroiderer, in blue, and in purple, in scarlet, and in fine linen, and of the weaver, *even* of them that do any work, and of those that devise cunning work.

³⁶:¹Then wrought Bezaleel and Aholiab, and every wise hearted man, in whom the LORD put wisdom and understanding to know _____ to work all manner of work for the service of the sanctuary, according to all that the LORD had commanded. ²And Moses called Bezaleel and Aholiab, and every wise hearted man, in whose heart the LORD had put wisdom, *even* every one whose heart stirred him up to come unto the work to do it: ³And they received of Moses all the offering, which the children of Israel had brought for the work of the service of the sanctuary, to make it *withal.* And they brought yet unto him _____ offerings every morning. ⁴And all the wise men, that wrought all the work of the sanctuary, came every man from his work which they made;

⁵And they spake unto Moses, saying, The _____ _____ much _____ than _____ for the _____ of the _____, which the LORD commanded to make. ⁶And Moses gave commandment, and they caused it to be proclaimed throughout the camp, saying, Let neither man nor woman make any more work for the offering of the sanctuary. So the people were restrained from bringing. ⁷For the stuff they had was _____ for all the work to make it, and _____ _____.

⁸And every wise hearted man among them that wrought the work of the tabernacle made ten curtains *of* fine twined linen, and blue, and purple, and scarlet: *with* cherubims of cunning work made he them. ⁹The length of one curtain *was* twenty and eight cubits, and the breadth of one curtain four cubits: the curtains *were* all of one size. ¹⁰And he coupled the five curtains one unto another: and *the other* five curtains he coupled one unto another. ¹¹And he made loops of blue on the edge of one curtain from the selvedge in the coupling: likewise he made in the uttermost side of *another* curtain, in the coupling of the second. ¹²Fifty loops made he in one curtain, and fifty loops made he in the edge of the curtain which *was* in the coupling of the second: the loops held one *curtain* to another. ¹³And he made fifty taches of gold, and coupled the curtains one unto another with the taches: so it became one tabernacle.

¹⁴And he made curtains *of* goats' *hair* for the tent over the tabernacle: eleven curtains he made them. ¹⁵The length of one curtain *was* thirty cubits, and four cubits *was* the breadth of one curtain: the eleven curtains *were* of one size. ¹⁶And he coupled five curtains by themselves, and six curtains by themselves. ¹⁷And he made fifty loops upon the uttermost edge of the curtain in the coupling, and fifty loops made he upon the edge of the curtain which coupleth the second. ¹⁸And he made fifty taches *of* brass to couple the tent together, that it might be one. ¹⁹And he made a covering for the tent *of* rams' skins dyed red, and a covering *of* badgers' skins above *that.*

²⁰And he made boards for the tabernacle *of* shittim wood, standing up. ²¹The length of a board *was* ten cubits, and the breadth of a board one cubit and a half. ²²One board had two tenons, equally distant one from another: thus did he make for all the boards of the tabernacle. ²³And he made boards for the tabernacle; twenty boards for the south side southward: ²⁴And forty sockets of silver he made under the twenty boards; two sockets under one board for his two tenons, and two sockets under another board for his two tenons. ²⁵And for the other side of the tabernacle, *which is* toward the north corner, he

made twenty boards, 26And their forty sockets of silver; two sockets under one board, and two sockets under another board. 27And for the sides of the tabernacle westward he made six boards. 28And two boards made he for the corners of the tabernacle in the two sides. 29And they were coupled beneath, and coupled together at the head thereof, to one ring: thus he did to both of them in both the corners. 30And there were eight boards; and their sockets *were* sixteen sockets of silver, under every board two sockets.

31And he made bars of shittim wood; five for the boards of the one side of the tabernacle, 32And five bars for the boards of the other side of the tabernacle, and five bars for the boards of the tabernacle for the sides westward. 33And he made the middle bar to shoot through the boards from the one end to the other. 34And he overlaid the boards with gold, and made their rings *of* gold *to be* places for the bars, and overlaid the bars with gold.

35And he made a vail *of* blue, and purple, and scarlet, and fine twined linen: *with* cherubims made he it of cunning work. 36And he made thereunto four pillars *of* shittim *wood,* and overlaid them with gold: their hooks *were of* gold; and he cast for them four sockets of silver.

37And he made an hanging for the tabernacle door *of* blue, and purple, and scarlet, and fine twined linen, of needlework; 38And the five pillars of it with their hooks: and he overlaid their chapiters and their fillets with gold: but their five sockets *were of* brass.

37:1And Bezaleel made the ark *of* shittim wood: two cubits and a half *was* the length of it, and a cubit and a half the breadth of it, and a cubit and a half the height of it: 2And he overlaid it with pure gold within and without, and made a crown of gold to it round about. 3And he cast for it four rings of gold, *to be set* by the four corners of it; even two rings upon the one side of it, and two rings upon the other side of it. 4And he made staves *of* shittim wood, and overlaid them with gold. 5And he put the staves into the rings by the sides of the ark, to bear the ark.

6And he made the mercy seat *of* pure gold: two cubits and a half *was* the length thereof, and one cubit and a half the breadth thereof. 7And he made two _____ *of* gold, beaten out of one piece made he them, on the two ends of the mercy seat; 8One cherub on the end on this side, and another cherub on the *other* end on that side: out of the mercy seat made he the cherubims on the two ends thereof. 9And the cherubims spread out *their* _____ on high, *and* covered with their wings over the mercy seat, with their faces one to another; *even* to the mercy seatward were the faces of the cherubims.

10And he made the table of shittim wood: two cubits *was* the length thereof, and a cubit the breadth thereof, and a cubit and a half the height thereof: 11And he overlaid it with pure gold, and made thereunto a crown of gold round about. 12Also he made thereunto a border of an handbreadth round about; and made a crown of gold for the border thereof round about. 13And he cast for it four rings of gold, and put the rings upon the four corners that *were* in the four feet thereof. 14Over against the border were the rings, the places for the staves to bear the table. 15And he made the staves *of* shittim wood, and overlaid them with gold, to bear the table. 16And he made the vessels which *were* upon the table, his dishes, and his spoons, and his bowls, and his covers to cover withal, *of* pure gold.

17And he made the candlestick *of* pure gold: *of* beaten work made he the candlestick; his shaft, and his branch, his bowls, his knops, and his flowers, were of the same: 18And six branches going out of the sides thereof; three branches of the candlestick out of the one side thereof, and three branches of the candlestick out of the other side thereof: [19]Three bowls made after the fashion of almonds in one branch, a knop and a flower; and three bowls made like almonds in another branch, a knop and a flower: so throughout the six branches going out of the candlestick. [20]And in the candlestick *were* four bowls made like almonds, his knops, and his flowers: [21]And a knop under two branches of the same, and a knop under two branches of the same, and a knop under two branches of the same, according to the six branches going out of it. [22]Their knops and their branches were of the same: all of it *was* one beaten work *of* pure gold. [23]And he made his seven lamps, and his snuffers, and his snuffdishes, *of* pure gold. [24]*Of* a talent of pure gold made he it, and all the vessels thereof.

[25]And he made the incense altar *of* shittim wood: the length of it *was* a cubit, and the breadth of it a cubit; it *was* foursquare; and two cubits *was* the height of it; the horns thereof were of the same. [26]And he overlaid it with pure gold, *both* the top of it, and the sides thereof round about, and the horns of it: also he made unto it a crown of gold round about. [27]And he made two rings of gold for it under the crown thereof, by the two corners of it, upon the two sides thereof, to be places for the staves to bear it withal. [28]And he made the staves *of* shittim wood, and overlaid them with gold.

[29]And he made the holy anointing oil, and the pure incense of sweet spices, according to the work of the apothecary.

[38:1]And he made the altar of burnt offering *of* shittim wood: five cubits *was* the length thereof, and five cubits the breadth thereof; *it was* foursquare; and three cubits the height thereof. [2]And he made the horns thereof on the four corners of it; the horns thereof were of the same: and he overlaid it with _____. [3]And he made all the vessels of the altar, the pots, and the shovels, and the basons, *and* the fleshhooks, and the firepans: all the vessels thereof made he *of* brass. [4]And he made for the altar a brasen grate of network under the compass thereof beneath unto the midst of it. [5]And he cast four rings for the four ends of the grate of brass, *to be* places for the staves. [6]And he made the staves *of* shittim wood, and overlaid them with brass. [7]And he put the staves into the rings on the sides of the altar, to bear it withal; he made the altar hollow with boards.

[8]And he made the laver *of* brass, and the foot of it *of* brass, of the _____ of *the women* assembling, which assembled *at* the door of the tabernacle of the congregation.

[9]And he made the court: on the south side southward the hangings of the court *were of* fine twined linen, an hundred cubits: [10]Their pillars *were* twenty, and their brasen sockets twenty; the hooks of the pillars and their fillets *were of* silver. [11]And for the north side *the hangings were* an hundred cubits, their pillars *were* twenty, and their sockets of brass twenty; the hooks of the pillars and their fillets *of* silver. [12]And for the west side *were* hangings of fifty cubits, their pillars ten, and their sockets ten; the hooks of the pillars and their fillets *of* silver. [13]And for the east side eastward fifty cubits. [14]The hangings of the one side *of the gate were* fifteen cubits; their pillars three, and their sockets three. [15]And for the other side of the court gate, on this hand and that hand, *were* hangings of fifteen cubits; their pillars three, and their sockets three. [16]All the hangings of the court round about *were* of fine twined linen. [17]And the sockets for the pillars *were of* brass; the hooks of the pillars and their fillets *of* silver; and the overlaying of their chapiters *of* silver; and all the pillars of the court *were* filleted with silver. [18]And the hanging for the gate of the court *was* needlework, *of* blue, and purple, and scarlet, and fine twined linen: and twenty

cubits *was* the length, and the height in the breadth *was* five cubits, answerable to the hangings of the court. [19]And their pillars *were* four, and their sockets *of* brass four; their hooks *of* silver, and the overlaying of their chapiters and their fillets *of* silver. [20]And all the pins of the tabernacle, and of the court round about, *were of* brass.

[21]This is the sum of the tabernacle, *even* of the tabernacle of testimony, as it was counted, according to the commandment of Moses, *for* the service of the Levites, by the hand of Ithamar, son to Aaron the priest. [22]And Bezaleel the son of Uri, the son of Hur, of the tribe of Judah, made all that the LORD commanded Moses. [23]And with him *was* Aholiab, son of Ahisamach, of the tribe of Dan, an engraver, and a cunning workman, and an embroiderer in blue, and in purple, and in scarlet, and fine linen. [24]All the gold that was occupied for the work in all the work of the holy *place,* even the gold of the offering, was twenty and nine talents, and seven hundred and thirty shekels, after the shekel of the sanctuary. [25]And the silver of them that were numbered of the congregation *was* an hundred talents, and a thousand seven hundred and threescore and fifteen shekels, after the shekel of the sanctuary: [26]A bekah for every man, *that is,* half a shekel, after the shekel of the sanctuary, for every one that went to be numbered, from twenty years old and upward, for _____ hundred thousand and _____ thousand and _____ hundred and _____ men. [27]And of the hundred talents of silver were cast the sockets of the sanctuary, and the sockets of the vail; an hundred sockets of the hundred talents, a talent for a socket. [28]And of the thousand seven hundred seventy and five *shekels* he made hooks for the pillars, and overlaid their chapiters, and filleted them. [29]And the brass of the offering *was* seventy talents, and two thousand and four hundred shekels. [30]And therewith he made the sockets to the door of the tabernacle of the congregation, and the brasen altar, and the brasen grate for it, and all the vessels of the altar, [31]And the sockets of the court round about, and the sockets of the court gate, and all the pins of the tabernacle, and all the pins of the court round about.

[39:1]And of the blue, and purple, and scarlet, they made cloths of service, to do service in the holy *place,* and made the holy garments for Aaron; as the LORD commanded Moses. [2]And he made the ephod *of* gold, blue, and purple, and scarlet, and fine twined linen. [3]And they did beat the gold into thin plates, and cut *it into* wires, to work *it* in the blue, and in the purple, and in the scarlet, and in the fine linen, *with* cunning work. [4]They made shoulderpieces for it, to couple *it* together: by the two edges was it coupled together. [5]And the curious girdle of his ephod, that *was* upon it, *was* of the same, according to the work thereof; *of* gold, blue, and purple, and scarlet, and fine twined linen; as the LORD commanded Moses.

[6]And they wrought onyx stones inclosed in ouches of gold, graven, as signets are graven, with the names of the children of Israel. [7]And he put them on the shoulders of the ephod, *that they should be* stones for a memorial to the children of Israel; as the LORD commanded Moses.

[8]And he made the breastplate *of* cunning work, like the work of the ephod; *of* gold, blue, and purple, and scarlet, and fine twined linen. [9]It was foursquare; they made the breastplate double: a span *was* the length thereof, and a span the breadth thereof, *being* doubled. [10]And they set in it four rows of stones: *the first* row *was* a _____, a _____, and a _____: this *was* the _____ row. [11]And the _____ row, an _____, a _____, and a _____. [12]And the _____ row, a _____, an _____, and an _____. [13]And the

_____row, a _____, an _____, and a _____: *they were* inclosed in ouches of _____in their inclosings. ¹⁴And the stones *were* according to the names of the children of Israel, _____, according to their _____, *like* the engravings of a signet, every one with his name, according to the twelve tribes. ¹⁵And they made upon the breastplate chains at the ends, *of* wreathen work *of* pure gold. ¹⁶And they made two ouches *of* gold, and two gold rings; and put the two rings in the two ends of the breastplate. ¹⁷And they put the two wreathen chains of gold in the two rings on the ends of the breastplate. ¹⁸And the two ends of the two wreathen chains they fastened in the two ouches, and put them on the shoulderpieces of the ephod, before it. ¹⁹And they made two rings of gold, and put *them* on the two ends of the breastplate, upon the border of it, which *was* on the side of the ephod inward. ²⁰And they made two *other* golden rings, and put them on the two sides of the ephod underneath, toward the forepart of it, over against the *other* coupling thereof, above the curious girdle of the ephod. ²¹And they did bind the breastplate by his rings unto the rings of the ephod with a lace of blue, that it might be above the curious girdle of the ephod, and that the breastplate might not be loosed from the ephod; as the LORD commanded Moses.

²²And he made the robe of the ephod *of* woven work, all *of* blue. ²³And *there was* an hole in the midst of the robe, as the hole of an habergeon, *with* a band round about the hole, that it should not _____. ²⁴And they made upon the hems of the robe pomegranates *of* blue, and purple, and scarlet, *and* twined *linen.* ²⁵And they made bells *of* pure gold, and put the bells between the pomegranates upon the hem of the robe, round about between the pomegranates; ²⁶A bell and a pomegranate, a bell and a pomegranate, round about the hem of the robe to minister *in;* as the LORD commanded Moses.

²⁷And they made coats *of* fine linen *of* woven work for Aaron, and for his sons, ²⁸And a mitre *of* fine linen, and goodly bonnets *of* fine linen, and linen breeches *of* fine twined linen, ²⁹And a girdle *of* fine twined linen, and blue, and purple, and scarlet, *of* needlework; as the LORD commanded Moses.

³⁰And they made the plate of the holy crown *of* pure gold, and wrote upon it a writing, *like to* the engravings of a signet, _____ TO THE _____. ³¹And they tied unto it a lace of blue, to fasten *it* on high upon the mitre; as the LORD commanded Moses.

³²Thus was all the work of the tabernacle of the tent of the congregation _____: and the children of Israel did according to _____ that the LORD commanded Moses, so did they.

³³And they brought the tabernacle unto Moses, the tent, and all his furniture, his taches, his boards, his bars, and his pillars, and his sockets, ³⁴And the covering of rams' skins dyed red, and the covering of badgers' skins, and the vail of the covering, ³⁵The ark of the testimony, and the staves thereof, and the mercy seat, ³⁶The table, *and* all the vessels thereof, and the shewbread, ³⁷The pure candlestick, *with* the lamps thereof, *even with* the lamps to be set in order, and all the vessels thereof, and the oil for light, ³⁸And the golden altar, and the anointing oil, and the sweet incense, and the hanging for the tabernacle door, ³⁹The brasen altar, and his grate of brass, his staves, and all his vessels, the laver and his foot, ⁴⁰The hangings of the court, his pillars, and his sockets, and the hanging for the court gate, his cords, and his pins, and all the vessels of the service of the tabernacle, for the tent of the congregation, ⁴¹The cloths of service to do service in the holy *place,* and the holy garments for Aaron the priest, and his sons' garments, to minister in the priest's office. ⁴²According to _____ that the LORD commanded Moses, so the

children of Israel made all the work. ⁴³And Moses did look upon all the work, and, behold, they have done it _____ the LORD had commanded, even so had they done it: and Moses _____ them.

⁴⁰:¹And the LORD spake unto Moses, saying, ²On the first day of the first month shalt thou set up the tabernacle of the tent of the congregation. ³And thou shalt put therein the ark of the testimony, and cover the ark with the vail. ⁴And thou shalt bring in the table, and set in order the things that are to be set in order upon it; and thou shalt bring in the candlestick, and light the lamps thereof. ⁵And thou shalt set the altar of gold for the incense before the ark of the testimony, and put the hanging of the door to the tabernacle. ⁶And thou shalt set the altar of the burnt offering before the door of the tabernacle of the tent of the congregation. ⁷And thou shalt set the laver between the tent of the congregation and the altar, and shalt put water therein. ⁸And thou shalt set up the court round about, and hang up the hanging at the court gate. ⁹And thou shalt take the anointing oil, and anoint the tabernacle, and all that *is* therein, and shalt hallow it, and all the vessels thereof: and it shall be _____. ¹⁰And thou shalt anoint the altar of the burnt offering, and all his vessels, and sanctify the altar: and it shall be an altar _____ holy. ¹¹And thou shalt anoint the laver and his foot, and sanctify it. ¹²And thou shalt bring Aaron and his sons unto the door of the tabernacle of the congregation, and wash them with water. ¹³And thou shalt put upon Aaron the holy garments, and anoint him, and sanctify him; that he may minister unto me in the priest's office. ¹⁴And thou shalt bring his sons, and clothe them with coats: ¹⁵And thou shalt anoint them, as thou didst anoint their father, that they may minister unto me in the priest's office: for their anointing shall surely be an everlasting priesthood throughout their generations. ¹⁶Thus did Moses: according to all that the LORD commanded him, so did he.

¹⁷And it came to pass in the first month in the second year, on the first *day* of the month, *that* the tabernacle was reared up. ¹⁸And Moses reared up the tabernacle, and fastened his sockets, and set up the boards thereof, and put in the bars thereof, and reared up his pillars. ¹⁹And he spread abroad the tent over the tabernacle, and put the covering of the tent above upon it; as the LORD commanded Moses.

²⁰And he took and put the testimony into the ark, and set the staves on the ark, and put the mercy seat above upon the ark: ²¹And he brought the ark into the tabernacle, and set up the vail of the covering, and covered the ark of the testimony; as the LORD commanded Moses.

²²And he put the table in the tent of the congregation, upon the side of the tabernacle northward, without the vail. ²³And he set the bread in order upon it before the LORD; as the LORD had commanded Moses.

²⁴And he put the candlestick in the tent of the congregation, over against the table, on the side of the tabernacle southward. ²⁵And he lighted the lamps before the LORD; as the LORD commanded Moses.

²⁶And he put the golden altar in the tent of the congregation before the vail: ²⁷And he burnt sweet incense thereon; as the LORD commanded Moses.

²⁸And he set up the hanging *at* the door of the tabernacle. ²⁹And he put the altar of burnt offering *by* the door of the tabernacle of the tent of the congregation, and offered upon it the burnt offering and the meat offering; as the LORD commanded Moses.

³⁰And he set the laver between the tent of the congregation and the altar, and put water there, to wash *withal*. ³¹And Moses and Aaron and his sons washed their hands and their

feet thereat: ³²When they went into the tent of the congregation, and when they came near unto the altar, they _____; as the LORD commanded Moses. ³³And he reared up the court round about the tabernacle and the altar, and set up the hanging of the court gate. So Moses _____ the _____.

³⁴Then a cloud covered the tent of the congregation, and the _____ of the LORD _____ the tabernacle. ³⁵And Moses was not able to enter into the tent of the congregation, because the cloud abode thereon, and the _____ of the LORD _____ the tabernacle. ³⁶And when the cloud was taken _____ from over the tabernacle, the children of Israel _____ onward in all their journeys: ³⁷But if the cloud were _____ taken up, then they journeyed _____ till the day that it was taken up. ³⁸For the _____ of the LORD *was* upon the tabernacle by _____, and _____ was on it by _____, in the sight of all the house of Israel, throughout all their journeys.

Made in the USA
Columbia, SC
19 June 2025